MW01025721

The Rights of Catholics in the Church

The Rights of Catholics in the Church

James A. Coriden

Paulist Press
New York/Mahwah, NJ

Cover design by Joy Taylor

Book design by Celine M. Allen

Library of Congress Cataloging-in-Publication Data

Coriden, James A.
    The rights of Catholics in the church / James A. Coriden.
        p. cm.
Includes bibliographical references and index.
    ISBN-13: 978-0-8091-4433-4 (alk. paper)
    1. Catholic Church—Membership. 2. Catholic Church—Doctrines. 3. Laity—Catholic Church. I. Title.
    BX1753.C61 2007
    262.9—dc22

                                                                2006022861

Published by Paulist Press
997 Macarthur Boulevard
Mahwah, New Jersey 07430

www.paulistpress.com

Printed and bound in the
United States of America

Contents

PART TWO
THE RIGHTS OF CATHOLICS IN THE CHURCH

PART THREE
LIMITATIONS ON AND DEFENSE OF
RIGHTS IN THE CHURCH

Abbreviations

AA   *Apostolicam Actuositatem,* decree of the Second Vatican Council on the apostolate of the laity, November 18, 1965

c.   canon (from the 1983 Code of Canon Law, unless otherwise indicated)

cc.   canons (from the 1983 Code of Canon Law, unless otherwise indicated)

CCEO   Code of Canons of the Eastern Churches, issued by John Paul II, October 18, 1990

CD   *Christus Dominus,* decree of the Second Vatican Council on the pastoral office of bishops, October 28, 1965

DH   *Dignitatis Humanae,* declaration of the Second Vatican Council on religious freedom, December 7, 1965

DV   *Dei Verbum,* dogmatic constitution of the Second Vatican Council on divine revelation, November 18, 1965

FC   *Familiaris Consortio,* apostolic exhortation of John Paul II on the role of the Christian family in the modern world, November 22, 1981

GE   *Gravissimum Educationis*, declaration of the Second
          Vatican Council on Christian education, October 28,
          1965

GS   *Gaudium et Spes*, pastoral constitution of the Second
          Vatican Council on the church in the modern world,
          December 7, 1965

HV   *Humanae Vitae*, encyclical letter of Paul VI on the
          regulation of birth, July 25, 1968

LG   *Lumen Gentium*, dogmatic constitution of the Second
          Vatican Council on the church, November 21, 1964

n.   number

PO   *Presbyterorum Ordinis*, decree of the Second Vatican
          Council on the ministry and life of priests, December
          7, 1965

SC   *Sacrosanctum Concilium*, constitution of the Second
          Vatican Council on the sacred liturgy, December 4,
          1963

UR   *Unitatis Redintegratio*, decree of the Second Vatican
          Council on ecumenism, November 21, 1964

Introduction

This book attempts to describe and explain the rights that Roman Catholics have as members of their church. It is a basic reference for those who want to know about or pursue their rights as Catholics.

The aim of a book on the rights of Catholics is to enhance the sense of justice and fairness within the church community. The mission of the church is advanced when its inner life is regulated by respect and love. The aim of a book that insists on rights is not to foster individualism, for the church is communitarian by nature, but rather to increase the sense of rightful belonging and full participation in the members of the church, especially the laity.

I hope that the book will appeal to those actively involved in the church: parish council members, parish staff, committee members, religion teachers, official ministers, volunteers in ministry, church employees, and ordinary Catholics who might wonder if they have any rights as parishioners.

The book is written in straightforward language and without footnotes. It contains explicit references to the sources of the rights, and it concludes with suggestions for further reading. This is a reference book on rights. Its purpose is to avoid litigation, not to promote it, to reduce conflicts, not to stimulate them.

The focus here is on the lay members of the Roman Catholic Church, because the laity seem most in need of knowledge about their rights, but the rights outlined in the book apply equally to all Catholics, including deacons, priests, bishops, and members of religious communities. The term "faithful" is often used here to describe those who are baptized and believing members of the church; it is a term of profound respect.

The context of the book is the United States, but it should be intelligible to and helpful for those in other parts of the world, because the rights described are universal, that is, they are based on the norms and teachings of the universal church. Likewise, the emphasis is on the Latin or Western Catholic Church, but the rights are equally applicable to those in the eastern or Oriental churches in union with Rome.

The rights that are described in the book, some twenty-eight of them, are some but not all of the rights that Catholics have as Catholics. There are many others, taken quite for granted and uncontested, that are not mentioned here, such as the rights to pray, to participate in the liturgy of the hours, to contribute to the church, to make a bequest in favor of the church, to serve as sponsor at baptism or confirmation or a witness at marriage, to give testimony in church trials, and many more.

There are other rights, basic human rights, that are not treated explicitly here because people do not usually look to the church to provide or guarantee them. Examples of such rights include the most fundamental right of all, the right to life, as well as the rights to food, clothing, shelter, education, and personal safety. We expect the church to teach and honor these rights, to assist in providing them when that is necessary, and certainly not to jeopardize them, but we don't think it is the church's primary responsibility to provide them.

Many of the rights of Catholics are stated in the Code of Canon Law. "Canon law" is the name for the church's own sys-

tem of regulations, its rules of discipline. The current Code of
Canon Law was issued by Pope John Paul II in 1983. It contains
1,752 "canons," that is, rules or norms applicable to the entire
Latin or Western church everywhere in the world. The Oriental
churches are governed by the Code of Canons of the Eastern
Churches issued by the same pope in 1990. The rights of the
faithful make up a very significant part of these two church
rulebooks.

Some of the rights of Catholics are not explicitly stated in
the codes. They are based instead on the *teachings* of the
church, rather than on its disciplinary or legal documents. There
are many more teaching documents—such as the constitutions
and decrees of the Second Vatican Council (1962–1965), the encyclicals of the popes, the pastoral letters of bishops—than there
are legal or "canonical" (canon law) documents. The church
takes its teaching documents very seriously, and they can be a
source of rights.

There are many case studies throughout this book. Some are
factual, others are based on actual happenings with certain elements changed, and some are purely fictional. The cases are included here not as history, but simply as illustrations of the
rights being discussed in the text. Often the cases are negative
examples, instances where the rights claimed were not achieved.
In that sense, they reveal the present reality. They demonstrate
the as-yet-unrealized state of rights in the church.

This book is divided into three parts. Part one presents in-
troductory chapters on the meaning of rights in the Catholic
Church and who possesses those rights.

Part two addresses the rights themselves, clustered into six
categories:

1. rights of membership,

2. rights to word, sacraments, and pastoral care,

3. rights to initiatives and activities,

4. rights related to one's state of life,

5. rights to formation and education, and

6. rights to due process.

Part three contains concluding chapters that deal with limitations on the exercise of rights in the church and ways to defend or vindicate one's rights in the church.

When Pope John Paul II promulgated the Code of Canon Law in 1983 he wrote of the reasons why the Code is extremely necessary for the church. "The Church must have norms...in order that the mutual relations of the faithful may be regulated according to justice based on charity, *with the rights of individuals guaranteed and well-defined*" (apostolic constitution, *Sacrae Disciplinae Leges,* January 25, 1983; emphasis added).

I hope that this small book may help to make those rights better known and understood, and given greater respect.

The Spirit of God, who directs the course of the ages and renews the face of the earth, is present in the evolution of personal dignity, human rights, and an order based on truth, justice, love, and freedom (*GS* 26). I pray that the empowering Spirit will make that same order evolve and flourish in the church.

I

AN OVERVIEW OF
RIGHTS IN THE CHURCH

WHAT DO WE MEAN
BY RIGHTS IN THE CHURCH?

Christian Freedom

Freedom is central to Christianity. Jesus spoke of the freedom of those who believe in him: "If you continue in my word, you are truly my disciples; and you will know the truth, and the truth will make you free" (John 8:31–32).

The Apostle Paul used the idea of freedom to describe the saving action of Christ. He contrasted the free status of the followers of Christ to the enslaved condition of those who preceded Christ: "For freedom Christ has set us free. Stand firm therefore, and do not submit again to a yoke of slavery" (Gal 5:1). Paul referred to freedom from the Mosaic law, from sin, and from death, three different sources of enslavement. "The law of the spirit of life in Christ Jesus has set you free from the law of sin and death" (Rom 8:2).

The presence of the Holy Spirit, given to every Christian at baptism, guarantees this Christian freedom: "Where the Spirit of the Lord is, there is freedom" (2 Cor 3:17). Those who are led by the Spirit are no longer subject to the law of Moses. The indwelling Spirit replaces a subjection to the extrinsic norms of the law (Gal 5:18). For Paul then, the Christian vocation is a call to liberty.

The Letter of James refers to the saving word of Christ as "the perfect law, the law of liberty" (Jas 1:25). It makes Christians doers of the word, and not hearers only. Freedom is central to the new law, the law of grace. It is not only freedom *from* an old law, which hindered rather than helped; it is a freedom *for* service and Christ-like love.

Rights within the church must be viewed in the context of Christian freedom. Rights mark the parameters of freedom of the faithful within in the life of the church. The rights of the baptized are the markers that outline a large zone of freedom of belief and action. Rights function as empowerments for the faithful to carry out their Christian vocation, as freedoms to enable them to fulfill their calling.

The Catholic Church and Rights

The Roman Catholic Church is a major force within the whole Christian movement. It is the largest of the Christian churches, with over a billion members all over the globe, and its history traces back to the time of Christ. Has the Catholic Church distinguished itself for its concern about the rights of its members over all those centuries? Not always. Although the church fiercely defended its own rights against Roman emperors, medieval kings, and modern dictators, and in doing so preserved and enhanced the rights and freedoms of its members, still it was the well-being of the church as a corporate entity that was at the heart of the ongoing struggle for Christian liberty.

However, the church's own legal system, canon law, which was organized and developed in the eleventh to thirteenth centuries, gave serious attention to personal rights. The canonical collections and commentaries of the Middle Ages were filled with clarifications of rights and duties and the procedures to pursue them. Most of the rules pertained to the clergy and religious; there was no listing of specific rights for members of the church. But the medieval canonists had a keen concern for justice and developed a system of individual and collective rights. In fact, this development long pre-dates the works on individual rights by the celebrated secular writers of the seventeenth and eighteenth centuries.

The church's first Code of Canon Law, a concise summary of canonical rules issued in 1917, showed respect for the rights of the baptized, but these rights were more often implied than explicitly stated. The 1917 Code, which contained 2,414 canons (rules), gave broad and explicit recognition to the rights of the laity in only one canon: The laity have the right to receive from the clergy the spiritual goods of the church and especially the means necessary for salvation (1917 Code, c. 682).

In this code there was no "bill of rights" for church members, but their rights were recognized indirectly in many ways. Many of the obligations of clerical office-holders (pastors, bishops) were imposed in order to safeguard the rights of the people; examples include the duty of residing within the parish or diocese (against absenteeism), and the obligations to offer Mass for their people every Sunday and holy day, to preach, and to teach.

The 1917 Code indicated many other rights of all baptized persons in its canons. It affirmed the rights of the faithful to join in associations and to assemble in pursuit of their goals. The people were assured free access to churches for sacred services. Availability of the sacraments of Holy Communion, penance, anointing of the sick, and marriage was clearly stated in the canons, as was access to Christian burial. The canons also prescribed just wages and fair treatment for church workers. Procedures for the defense or vindication of rights existed, even though they were inadequate in practice. A canon on the interpretation of laws illustrated the positive canonical attitude toward rights. It stated that any law that restricts the free exercise of rights must be interpreted strictly or narrowly (1917 Code, c. 19). In other words, the canonical tradition held that in principle human liberty should be minimally restricted.

The church's convictions about personal rights developed remarkably in the century following Pope Leo XIII's 1891 encyclical letter *On the Condition of Workers* (*Rerum Novarum*) in the context of the development of the church's social teaching. Pope John XXIII's 1963 encyclical letter, *Peace on Earth* (*Pacem in Terris*), and the Second Vatican Council's 1965 *Pastoral Constitution on the Church in the Modern World* (*Gaudium et Spes*) articulated and endorsed a whole range of fundamental human rights based on the sublime dignity of the human person. For example, one passage from the council document states:

> There must be made available to all everything necessary for leading a truly human life, such as food, clothing, and shelter, the right to choose a state of life freely and to found a family, the right to education, to work, to a good reputation, to respect, to appropriate information, to act in accord with the right norm of conscience, to the protection of privacy, and to rightful freedom, even in religious matters. (*GS* 26)

The church gradually realized that it must not only teach and preach on social justice and human rights, but also put them into practice in its own life. The 1971 Synod of Bishops declared that:

> while the church is bound to give witness to justice, it recognizes that anyone who ventures to speak to people about justice must first be just in their eyes. Hence we must undertake an examination of the modes of acting

and of the possessions and life-style found within the church itself.

Within the church rights must be preserved. No one should be deprived of his or her ordinary rights because he or she is associated with the church in one way or another. (*Justice in the World*, 40–41)

In other words, the church does not pretend to provide all of the basic human rights—food, clothing, shelter, employment—but at least people should not be deprived of those rights because they belong to or work for the church.

The 1983 Code of Canon Law

After the Second Vatican Council ended in 1965, the church began the process of revising its Code of Canon Law. As it did so, it adopted a set of "Principles to Direct the Revision of the Code," and the issue of rights emerged prominently among them: the Code must define and protect the rights and obligations of each person, it is expedient that the rights of persons be appropriately defined and safeguarded, it is necessary to develop procedures for the protection of subjective rights (preface to the 1983 Code).

Thus it was that the church's social teaching on rights entered into and influenced the church's own rules of discipline when, after a long process of composition and consultation, the revised Code of Canon Law was issued by Pope John Paul II in 1983.

For the first time in history, the new Code contained a "bill of rights" for all of the church's members. In addition to the many rights indirectly asserted and embedded in the obligations and duties of others, now there was a separate and prominent section of the Code on "The Obligations and Rights of All the Christian Faithful" (cc. 208–223). Fifteen specific rights of all the faithful were declared in these canons. Moreover, the new Code contained other statements of rights and duties for special groups of the faithful: laity (cc. 224–231), clergy (cc. 273–289), religious men and women (cc. 662–672). The era of explicit rights for Catholics in the church had arrived. Catholic canonists celebrated this development as a major breakthrough.

These canonical rights are explained in this book, as are other rights that are asserted or implied in the church's rules or teachings.

However, it is only fair to note that making these rights real is still a work in progress. Most Catholics are not aware of their rights, and some of those who know about them have been stymied in their efforts to have them respected. Adequate avenues to pursue these rights are largely lacking. This book is written precisely in order to advance the realization of rights in the church.

Categories of Rights

Rights in the church are commonly divided into four general categories based on their sources, that is, on their bases or roots.

1. Human rights are those derived from the nature and dignity of the human person. They are common to all persons as the rightful heritage of their humanity. They are the kinds of rights recognized in the United Nations *Universal Declaration of Human Rights* (1948) or like those mentioned in the council document quoted above (*GS* 26). These basic rights include the rights to life, liberty, equality, privacy, movement, marriage and family, freedom of thought, conscience and religion, opinion and expression, assembly and association, work, ownership of property, and education.

These fundamental human rights are not lost by a person's baptism into the church. They remain, and many of them are explicitly acknowledged by the church. It is not surprising that not *all* of these rights are stated in the church's rules, simply because no one expects the church to provide them, that is, they are not claims likely to arise within the community of the church. For instance, it is not usually the responsibility of the church to guarantee the right to ownership of private property, or to provide general education, or to assure freedom of movement, or to provide employment. Such neutral or secular human rights are usually within the jurisdiction of the state, rather than the church.

Some human rights are qualified or limited because of their exercise within the church. For example, while the canons recognize the right and duty of the faithful to make their opinions known to their pastors, the people are urged to do so keeping in mind the faith and moral teachings of the church and with reverence for their pastors (c. 212.3). Catholics can found or join associations for a wide range of purposes (c. 215), but they are not to direct, promote, or join those that plot against the church (c. 1372).

2. Ecclesial rights are those that accrue to the person in virtue of her or his baptism. These are rights of membership in the church (*ecclesia*), based on a person's full incorporation into the church and consequent participation in its mission.

Such rights include: access to the word of God and to the sacraments of the church (c. 213), the right to Christian formation (c. 217), the right to marry in the church (c. 1058), the right to one's own form of spiritual life (c. 214), and the right to Christian burial (c. 1176.1).

These rights too, even though they can be viewed as membership benefits, are not absolute or unqualified. For example, although access to the Eucharist is a basic right (c. 912), one who is conscious of grave sin is not to receive Holy Communion without first going to confession or making an act of perfect contrition (c. 916). Even though the right to marry is also very fundamental, those who are under age or are close blood relatives are prohibited from marrying in the church (cc. 1083, 1091).

3. Ecclesiastical rights are based on church law and apply to those who hold public office in the church, for example, pastors, chaplains, or bishops. Ecclesiastical or canonical rules grant certain rights, like decent remuneration for clerics (c. 281.1), stability in office for a pastor (c. 522), or the right of a diocesan bishop to establish parishes (c. 515.2), to appoint pastors (c. 523), and to convoke the diocesan pastoral council (c. 514.1). These rights are one way of describing the pastoral prerogatives that accrue to those holding office in the church.

4. Communal rights belong to individuals by virtue of their membership in communities or associations recognized by the church, such as religious communities of women or men or associations of the faithful. These rights are based on the law of the church for such groups or on the statutes of the groups themselves. For example, the members of associations of the faithful have the right to elect their own leaders, initiate their own endeavors, and administer their own goods (cc. 298–329). Members of religious communities have the right to the support and assistance they need to fulfill their vocation (c. 670); most have the right to elect their leadership, and the communities have the right to a certain autonomy of life, activities, and possessions (c. 586).

Qualities of Rights in the Church

Rights in the church are different from rights in secular society.
Rights are just claims or legal titles. Rights are defined as "powers of free action," and thus they are often called freedoms. The meaning of the word "rights" is qualified by the context in which it is used. Rights take on a different shade of meaning when they are asserted in civil society and in the community known as the church, because as a kind of society the state is very different from the church.

The church is a communion based on faith, on a firm belief in God's self-revelation in Jesus Christ. The church was co-constituted by Christ and the Holy Spirit, and it stands as the humble sacrament of God's presence in the world. The church is a communion of those who believe and are baptized, those who share at the table of the Lord, and who also share in carrying out the mission entrusted to the church on earth. In sociological terms, the church is a voluntary association, one that persons freely join and in which they freely remain. Rights within this communion of faith, grace, charism, and love take on a different coloration than rights within civil societies, cities, states, and nations.

Two passages in the New Testament illustrate this different attitude toward rights within the church. In the first, the Apostle Paul expresses indignation when he learns that members of the Christian community are bringing lawsuits against one another before pagan judges in Roman courts. "When any of you has a grievance against another, do you dare to take it to court before the unrighteous instead of taking it before the saints?... Can it be that there is no one among you wise enough to decide between one believer and another?" (1 Cor 6:1–5). In other words, the members of the Christian community are related to one another by the special bonds of communion, like the ties between brothers and sisters in the same family. If there are disputes or rights-claims between them, they should be settled "within the family," not by outsiders who do not belong to the family of faith.

A second instance is the three-stage procedure outlined in Matthew's Gospel for disciplining a wayward member of the community: personal confrontation, accusation before witnesses, and a hearing before the assembled community.

> If another member of the church sins against you, go and point out the fault when the two of you are alone. If the member listens to you, you have regained that one. But if you are not listened to, take one or two others along with you, so that every word may be confirmed by the evidence of two or three witnesses. If the member refuses to listen to them, tell it to the church; and if the offender refuses to listen even to the church, let such a one be to you as a Gentile and a tax collector. (Matt 18:15–17)

In other words, the offense is to be managed within the community of faith. If the offending members will not accept the judgment of the local congregation, then they are to be excluded, so that they will realize the error of their ways and repent. The point of the process is conversion and reconciliation within the communion of the church, not punishment and expulsion.

Rights in the church are always exercised in communion.
As the above two passages show, rights in the church are envisioned and claimed within the communion, just as the rights of citizens are envisioned and claimed within the state or nation. The communion of the church is the distinctive and necessary context for rights in the church.

Those Catholics in full communion with the church possess the Spirit of Christ, accept the church's structure and means of salvation, and are united with Christ by the bonds of faith, the sacraments, and governance (*LG* 14). They are obliged to maintain this communion with the church in the way they act (c. 209.1), even in the way that they look upon and exercise their rights.

On the part of the faithful, this implies a willingness to make compromises and concessions in the pursuit of rights. On the part of church authorities, it demands flexibility and accommodation so that those who feel their rights have been denied or violated are not driven out of the church.

Communion is the bond of unity that is the gift of the Holy Spirit. It must be preserved at all cost.

Another way of saying that communion is the necessary context for rights in the church is to describe rights in the church as communitarian rather than individualist. We possess and exercise rights in the church as members of communities (parishes, dioceses, religious orders), not simply as isolated individuals. We have a sense of belonging to a community first and foremost, and we are always conscious of how our actions will affect the community. Just as we pray in the first person plural (*our* Father, *we* believe, let *us* pray), so we think and act as a *community* of Christ's disciples, united in his Spirit.

The common good consists in safeguarding rights.
The common good of any society, including the church, consists in the array of social conditions that enable groups and individuals to develop themselves more fully and easily. This facilitation of development consists chiefly in the protection of the rights and the performance of the duties of the human person (*DH* 6). Thus the common good is achieved precisely in and through the exercise of rights and the fulfillment of responsibilities.

We in the church often lose sight of this important truth. The common good is sometimes viewed only as a counterweight or limitation to the exercise of rights. Indeed, the church's canons caution that the faithful, in exercising their rights, are to take into account the common good of the church, and that church authorities can moderate the exercise of rights in view of the common good (c. 223). This is frequently interpreted to mean that the common good of the church imposes necessary restrictions on the rights of the faithful, whereas the opposite is more often the case: the common good of the church is actually *fostered* by the exercise of rights and the performance of obligations on the part of the faithful.

The common good of the church is to create and sustain local communities in which the faithful can hear and respond to the word of God, celebrate the sacraments and offer praise to God, grow into mature disciples of Christ, give witness to their faith, hope, and love, exercise their Spirit-given charisms and ministries, and rejoice in the communion of the people of God.

This overarching goal of the common good is facilitated and advanced by the exercise of the rights of the faithful, as described individually below, and by their fulfillment of their duties. As stated by the council, the principle of full freedom is that people are to be given the maximum of liberty, and restrained only when and insofar as necessary (*DH* 7). This principle also applies to rights in the church.

Rights imply corresponding duties.

Obligations are the other side of the coin of rights. In any society or organization, the rights of members imply corresponding duties. In civil society citizens enjoy various constitutional or legal rights, such as freedom of speech, freedom of religion, or freedom of movement, and in exchange they must fulfill certain obligations, such as the payment of taxes, obedience to laws, or service on juries.

It is the same way in the Catholic Church. Rights carry with them corresponding duties. For example, the right to remain in full communion with the church means that members are obliged to keep themselves in communion and to participate actively in the church's mission (c. 209). The right of the faithful to make their desires and opinions known to their pastoral leaders goes hand in hand with a duty to follow the teachings and leadership decisions of those same pastors (c. 212). The right to engage in spreading the gospel message by word and example is tied closely to the duty to do so (c. 211).

This is a book about the rights of Catholics in the church. A companion volume could be written about the obligations of Catholics in the church. The fact that the duties of Catholics receive only passing mention here does not mean that Catholics do not have such duties as members of the church, nor does it imply that their duties are not serious. Indeed, Catholics are often reminded of their very real obligations. They are simply not the main topic of this book.

WHO POSSESSES
RIGHTS IN THE CHURCH?

Those in Full Communion

Those who have been baptized and are in full communion with the Catholic Church possess rights in the church. The two key elements are *the sacrament of baptism* and *ecclesial communion*. "By baptism one is incorporated into the Church of Christ and is constituted a person in it with the duties and rights that are proper to Christians in keeping with their condition, insofar as they are in ecclesiastical communion..." (c. 96).

Legal personhood, that is, being recognized as a person in the church's legal system, being the subject of rights and duties, and having full legal standing, is defined in terms of baptism and communion. (Ecclesial communion is not the same as Holy Communion, but partaking of Holy Communion is the ultimate sign of being in ecclesial communion.)

"Those baptized are fully in the communion of the Catholic Church...who are joined with Christ in its visible structure by the bonds of the profession of faith, the sacraments, and church governance" (c. 205). They are fully incorporated into the church who possess the Spirit of Christ, accept the whole structure of the church and the means of salvation available within it, and who are united with Christ in the visible framework of the church by the three ties of faith, the sacraments, and governance (*LG* 14).

The term "condition" used in canon 96 quoted in the first paragraph of this chapter ("in keeping with their condition") refers to the categories of one's canonical status that can qualify one's rights in the church:

- age: infant, minor, or a person who has reached majority (cc. 97–98)

- use of reason: *sui compos* or *non sui compos*, i.e., habitually lacking the use of reason (c. 99)

- residence: domiciled in a parish or diocese or transient (cc. 100–107)

- marital state: single, married, separated (cc. 1055, 1134, 1141–1155)

- parenthood: having children, natural or adopted (c. 1136)

- vocational state: lay, ordained, member of a religious community (c. 207)

- rite: enrollment in a ritual church by baptism or transfer (cc. 111–112)

Each one of these conditions can modify the rights the persons possess and their ability to exercise them; for instance, minors are subject to their parents or guardians (c. 98.2).

There are several other categories of persons whose possession of rights in the Catholic Church merits special attention.

Converts

Those who were baptized in another Christian church and then joined the Catholic Church by means of a profession of faith and the reception of Holy Communion, whether they did so as children or adults, and whether they went through the Rite of Christian Initiation for Adults or not, are fully incorporated into the church. They are in full communion and enjoy the full measure of rights in the church.

Catechumens

Those who have asked to be incorporated into the church are already joined to the church in a special way. By their desire to enter the church and by their life of faith, hope, and charity, they are united to the church, and the church cherishes them as its own (c. 206.1). The church invites them to lead a gospel-inspired life, it introduces them to its worship rituals, and it grants them various prerogatives (c. 206.2), such as the right to a funeral in the church (c. 1183.1). However, catechumens have not yet been fully incorporated into the church, and thus do not possess the rights of those completely in communion. For example, they are not yet invited to the table of the Lord for Holy Communion.

Non-practicing Catholics

Those who were baptized into the Catholic Church or received into it after being baptized in another Christian denomination but who are no longer active in the practice of their faith are in a somewhat ambiguous situation. On one hand, they are technically still in full communion. "Once a Catholic, always a Catholic" is a canonical slogan. Their rights are legally intact. They are always welcome back to active participation in the church. They are not to be denied church funerals (c. 1184).

On the other hand, either they have distanced themselves from the life of the church or their circumstances have forced them to become inactive; in either case their bonds of communion with the church have been stretched thin. Their attempts to claim their rights within the community of the church may be greeted with skepticism if they are not preceded or accompanied by signs of return and revival of participation.

Sociological students of the church are wont to characterize parishioners as *nuclear* (most active), *modal* (ordinary members), *marginal* (rarely involved), or *dormant* (inactive). Here we speak of non-practicing Catholics, the dormant variety.

Former Catholics

Those who were at one time fully incorporated into the Catholic Church but who then departed from it and affiliated themselves with another Christian church or another religious faith are also in an ambiguous position regarding their rights in the Catholic Church. From a canonical point of view, they remain Catholics. They are still persons in and of the church, subjects of rights and duties (cc. 96, 11). They remain members of the family of faith.

If their departure from the Catholic Church involved a conscious and formal refusal of communion with the church, it could result in their excommunication. That carries with it not a total separation from the church but a serious restriction of their rights (cc. 751, 1364, 1331), such as the right to receive Holy Communion.

From an experiential point of view, such persons usually identify themselves with their new church or religion; they no longer sense themselves to be Catholics, and they are unlikely to attempt to vindicate their rights within the Catholic Church. However, they are not technically barred from trying to do so (c. 1476).

Non-Catholic Christians

Fellow Christians who have never been formally affiliated with the Catholic Church are related to the church by many elements of communion: acceptance of sacred scripture, belief in God the Father and in Christ as savior, baptism into Christ, the bond of the Holy Spirit from whom come gifts and graces, a life of faith, hope, and charity (*LG* 15, *UR* 3). Hence we speak of such persons as "in communion" with the Catholic Church, but not in *full* communion. They are not joined to its visible structure by the bonds of the profession of faith, the celebration of the sacraments, and the acceptance of the same ecclesiastical governance (c. 205). Therefore, they do not have legal personhood in the church, and they do not possess duties and rights within it (c. 96).

"Double Belonging"

Sometimes "mixed marriage" families, that is, those resulting from marriages between Catholics and baptized members of other Christian churches not in full communion with the Catholic Church (c. 1124), maintain active membership in both churches. As a matter of religious conviction or even as a micromodel of ecumenical witness, they attend worship services at

both churches and participate in the activities of both congregations. The phenomenon is referred to as "double belonging."

What is the rights situation of such families? There is no
doubt that the Catholic party remains a Catholic with all the
duties and rights that entails. Likewise, the couple's children
who are baptized in the Catholic Church are in full communion
with the church and possess all the rights and obligations of
Catholics. But what about the non-Catholic partner in the marriage, say the Methodist husband and father? If he has formally
joined the Catholic Church by a profession of faith and reception of Holy Communion, he is in full communion and enjoys
the rights and duties of a Catholic. However, if he has retained
his membership in his Methodist congregation and simply at-
tends Mass and other events with his Catholic spouse, then he
is not in full communion and does not possess the rights of a
Catholic.

The "double belonging" of interchurch families is an ad-
mirable ecumenical stance, and it may foreshadow the conver-
gence of the Christian churches. However, in the rights arena—
for instance, with regard to sacramental sharing and pastoral
care—it can sometimes entail rough going. The Catholic Church
has not yet made adequate provision for dual membership, and
these faith-filled families continue to challenge us.

II

THE RIGHTS OF CATHOLICS
IN THE CHURCH

1. RIGHTS OF MEMBERSHIP, OF BELONGING TO THE CHURCH

A. THE RIGHT TO COMMUNION WITH THE CHURCH

Explanation

The Christian faithful are *obliged* to maintain communion with the church (c. 209). The other side of this coin is their reciprocal *right* to maintain communion. In a way, this right to communion is the most radical of all of the rights of Catholics in the church.

"Communion" expresses the very warp and woof of the church, the reality that binds it together. Communion is the bond of unity whose source is the Holy Spirit. Communion describes first of all the sharing in God's own life by every one of the baptized.

Communion also means the bond of unity that links together all the elements of church: individuals, parishes, dioceses, national churches, ritual churches, regional churches, and the church universal. This linkage is not a static thing, like the chains that anchor ships to a wharf, but a vital force, like the bones, sinews, arteries, and nerves that make the body function as one living organism. The right and duty of communion implies being fully part of the church community.

"Full incorporation" in the church includes those who:
- possess the Spirit of Christ,
- accept the church's whole structure and means of salvation, and
- are united with Christ by the bonds of profession of faith, the sacraments, church governance, and communion (*LG* 14).

This incorporation is accomplished canonically by baptism (c. 96) and theologically and liturgically by all three sacraments of initiation (baptism, confirmation, and Eucharist). Once it is complete, communion is a right of belonging that can't be reversed except by the person's own initiative, that is, by a person's defection from the church, rejection of the faith (c. 751), or perpetration of a canonically serious crime. Even in these instances, the breaking of communion is only partial, and not total. To repeat the canonical adage, "Once a Catholic, always a Catholic." As in a family, they might not speak to you, but you're still part of the family.

The penalty of excommunication sounds as though one is cut off from communion with the church, but such is not the case. Excommunicated persons (c. 1331) may not take the sacraments or hold a church office as long as they are under that penalty, but they can always be fully reconciled to the church if they repent and promise to make reparation for any harm or scandal they have caused (cc. 1358, 1347.2). They remain in communion, but with attenuated rights.

CASE

Founded in 1888, Good Shepherd parish is located in the inner city. Father John Allan was ordained just two years when he was assigned as administrator to what seemed to be a dying parish community. It was down to about two hundred members. Father Allan stayed and led the parish for twenty-two years. In that time Good Shepherd grew in numbers to about three thousand. Even more remarkable was the parish's growth in dynamic activity and social outreach. It sponsored large and successful programs that provided food, clothing, medical care, and shelter for the poor. It welcomed people from other Christian denominations, and attracted many gay and lesbian Catholics. Good Shepherd's liturgies were lively and innovative, and the ministry of women was prominent.

Over the years, the bishop met several times with Father Allan regarding parish practices that many described as questionable. Three practices in particular were repeatedly mentioned as problematic: (1) inviting non-Catholics to receive the Eucharist, (2) blessing the unions of gay and lesbian persons, and (3) permitting a woman to stand at the altar beside the presiding celebrant, vested in alb and half stole, and reciting the canon of the Mass along with the celebrant.

In recent years the parish and its leader had been the targets of organized loyalist Catholics who denounced these practices as serious abuses. When the bishop did not take the corrective actions that the protesting groups demanded, they complained to congregations of the Roman Curia. The bishop received several inquiries from Rome regarding the ministry at Good Shepherd.

Finally, the bishop decided to remove Father Allan as administrator of Good Shepherd. The Sunday following the transfer, the bishop came to the Good Shepherd community and spoke to them about their identity as a Roman Catholic parish, and about their need to live according to the norms of the larger church. "The love of Jesus cannot be the sole criterion of membership here," he said.

The bishop named Father Murray as pastor of Good Shepherd, and a few days later he fired the woman pastoral associate who had often "concelebrated" Mass with Father Allan. Many parishioners were infuriated at these developments, and the new pastor's first celebration at the parish that weekend was marred by verbal insults.

Father Allan had been instructed to have no contact with the Good Shepherd community after his departure, but he returned to take part in liturgical celebrations. In December, when he refused to agree in writing not to repeat the practices that the bishop found objectionable, the bishop suspended him.

About a thousand of Good Shepherd's parishioners began to meet in a nearby Methodist church. Father Allan and the woman who had served as pastoral associate joined them. The group called themselves the New Flock Community. Their average weekly collection was $12,000, and they continued to support the social outreach ministries begun at Good Shepherd. About a thousand people remained at Good Shepherd with their pastor, Father Murray, and about another thousand left, going to other Catholic parishes or Protestant churches.

Six months later the chancellor of the diocese made the following announcement:

> The fact that a group of parishioners has broken away from the Roman Catholic Church is a matter of deep regret. Because of the importance of unity in the church, a schism, or separation, brings pain to the entire local church and our diocesan family. While we hope that unity may be restored, and want those who have separated from us to know that they are welcome to return, at this time we

must recognize that by starting this new church, a
schism has occurred.

Comment

Schism, which is defined in terms of a refusal or rejection of
communion with the rest of the church (c. 751), offends against
the unity of the church in the same way that divorce offends
against marriage. It is a great tragedy in the life of the church.
Despite good will and intense effort, hardened positions sometimes develop, and painful divisions can result, as they did in
this case. It represents a failure of both the obligation and the
right to maintain communion.

B. THE RIGHT TO PARTICIPATE ACTIVELY
IN THE LIFE OF THE CHURCH

Explanation

Every Catholic has the right to share fully in the life and activity
of the local church community. Everyone has the right to "a
place at the table," whether that means at the eucharistic table,
at the table of decision-making, or at the table of the gospel.

The principle of active participation is stated most clearly in
regard to the liturgy. The church wants all believers to take a
full, conscious, and active part in liturgical celebrations, whether
at Mass or at other sacramental rites. Active participation is demanded by the nature of the liturgy itself, and it is the right and
duty of Christian people in virtue of their baptism (SC 14).

This right to participate is based on each person's full incorporation into the church through reception of the sacraments of

initiation (baptism, confirmation, Eucharist), and the possession of the Holy Spirit. Those who are in full communion share in Christ's priestly, prophetic, and royal functions (c. 204.1), which means that they can and must take part in the sanctifying, teaching/learning, and pastoral roles of the church that carries on Christ's mission.

Since this right to share actively in the life of the church is rooted in the sacraments of membership, the scope of activities that it implies is very wide, much wider than active participation at Mass. It extends to matters of parish life and property, to programs and initiatives, to financial support and communications. It implies the right and duty to be fully engaged in the community.

The right of participation, like all other rights in the church, must be exercised with due regard for the common good (so the parish community can serve all its members) and for the rights of others. This right to active participation does not imply a right to dominate the parish, or to obstruct the development of valuable programs, or to divert resources to one's own personal interests. It gives the freedom to collaborate with one's fellow parishioners for the benefit of all, and calls for the very opposite of passivity and aloofness.

CASE

Father Ralph had been pastor of St. Joseph's parish for several years, but he sensed that things were not going well. He was worn out for one thing, and the people seemed less and less interested in parish activities.

Father Ralph thought of himself as the father of the parish family. He managed its affairs carefully and in detail, and pretty much by himself. He was a micro-manager.

An outside consultant was able to convince Father Ralph that a more collaborative leadership could both lighten his burdens and energize the parishioners.

Father Ralph went to the parish council and the other organizations within the parish and asked for their help in changing his style of pastoring. He stopped chairing the parish council, and he let the members set the agenda along with him. The same with the staff meetings. In both groups he allowed decisions to emerge by consensus and shared wisdom. Word spread, and parishioner interest and involvement began to rebound dramatically.

The consultant also recommended that Father Ralph hire a parish administrator to take care of the physical, financial, and personnel issues, so that he could focus more of his time and energy on spiritual and sacramental matters. He found a person in the parish who was experienced and efficient. She freed him of many time-consuming tasks, which she performed more professionally than he, and her work was much appreciated by the parishioners.

An encounter after Sunday Mass illustrates how Father Ralph's role and parishioner involvement had changed. A member of the parish angrily complained to him about the way that one of the minority groups in the parish was being neglected. Father Ralph calmed him down and said, "George, that's no longer my area. That issue belongs to the Committee on Community Life, and that woman over there is one of its members. She'll be happy to put it on their agenda."

Comment

There's nothing that stimulates participation more than meaningful involvement. When people feel that their presence and

opinions are taken seriously, it increases their sense of ownership of the community, and makes them want to stay involved.

In this case, the pastor took the initiative, but both he and
the people benefited from the change in his way of acting as
pastor. The community was enriched by the greater participation of its members.

C. THE RIGHT OF EQUALITY

Explanation

The Second Vatican Council firmly embraced the principle of
equality, both in the world at large and within the church.

> Since all men and women possessed of a rational soul
> and created in the image of God have the same nature
> and the same origin, and since they have been re-
> deemed by Christ and enjoy the same divine calling and
> destiny, the basic equality which they all share needs to
> be increasingly recognized. (GS 29)

> There is no inequality in Christ and in the church, with
> regard to race or nation, social condition or sex, because
> "there is neither Jew nor Greek, there is neither slave
> nor free, there is neither male nor female; for you are
> all one in Christ Jesus" (Gal 3, 28)...there is a true
> equality of all with regard to the dignity and action
> common to all the faithful concerning the building up
> of the body of Christ. (LG 32)

The principle of equality is spelled out in the church's rules,
specifically in the first of the canons on "The Obligations and

Rights of All the Christian Faithful" (cc. 208–223). Our radical equality within the church is sacramental, stemming as it does from our baptism into Christ. It is described as a true equality in the dignity and action by which we all cooperate in building up the body of Christ, the church (c. 208).

Our equality in the church is radical, but it is also qualified by our condition (e.g., child, adult, lay, religious, ordained) and our function (e.g., teacher, pastor, parent, missionary) in the church.

Equality, then, is the constitutional status of the faithful in the church, and recognition of this is all the more remarkable when we consider the many centuries of explicit *inequality*. The church inherited from the Roman Empire a structure of distinct social classes, estates, and orders; the church even described itself as "a society of unequals" (*societas inaequalium*). The acknowledgement of the fundamental equality of all its members based on baptism was a turnabout indeed!

CASE

Rosalio and Rosaria Carrillo attended a party in their neighborhood and overheard a conversation in which another couple was complaining that their daughter's wedding at St. Henry's Church had cost them over $10,000. The Carrillos looked at one another in alarm. St. Henry's was their parish, and their twenty-three-year-old daughter Lara was planning to marry within the next year. The parents had hoped that she would marry at St. Henry's, even though she had not attended Mass there or anywhere else for the past few years. Her fiancé, also a Catholic, was also non-practicing.

The Carrillos had told their daughter that they would do what they could toward financing the wedding. Knowing that $10,000 would be way beyond their means, they began to make plans for a wedding at home. One of Lara's friends was an evangelical minister, and he suggested to her that he could marry them in a nice ceremony in their back yard. And that's exactly what happened.

When Lara and her husband had their first child, they took her to St. Henry's to be baptized, but when she was four years old, they began attending their friend's evangelical church.

Comment

The overheard conversation may have been accurate, but it led to an unfortunate conclusion. In all likelihood, only a small part of the $10,000 went to St. Henry's, even if the stipends for the priest, organist, soloist, and rental of the parish hall were included. However, the impression was given that those with very limited financial means would be out of place trying to hold a wedding there, in their own parish. Public disclosure of the usual fees along with a notice about special accommodations for the less affluent might have helped to avoid the unintended alienation of the young couple.

The principle of equality has other applications in the church. Parishes have a right of equality, just as individuals do. Local communities of the faithful are equal in dignity, whether they are large and affluent or small and poor. Local congregations are often both viable and vital despite their remote locations and relatively small numbers.

The Vatican Council affirmed that even in small, poor, and scattered parishes God has called the people together in the Holy Spirit, Christ is truly present, and by his power the one, holy, catholic, and apostolic church is gathered (*LG* 26).

In times of shortages of priests there is a temptation to close or merge parishes that in other times no one would think of closing. And in making judgments about parish closings, great care must be taken so that large and wealthy parishes are not unfairly favored while smaller and poorer parishes suffer discrimination.

D. THE RIGHT TO EXPRESS NEEDS, DESIRES, AND OPINIONS

Explanation

Self-expression is a very basic human need, and for that reason freedom of expression is asserted in nearly every modern declaration of human rights. The Catholic Church too specifically acknowledges the right of expression.

The faithful are free to make known their needs, especially their spiritual ones, and their desires to the leaders of the church (c. 212.2). Moreover, the faithful have the right and sometimes also the duty to make known to their pastors (bishops, parish priests, lay ministers) their opinions on matters pertaining to the good of the church, and the right to make them known to other members of the faithful as well (c. 212.3). This manifestation of opinions by the faithful is conditioned by:

– the extent of their knowledge and competence,

– due regard for the integrity of faith and morals,

– respect for their pastors,

– consideration for the common good of the church, and

– respect for the dignity and reputation of others (c. 212.3).

This right of free expression reflects not only the personal dignity of individual members of the church but also the nature and needs of the church as a community. Communication within the church is necessary for its healthy functioning. Pope Pius XII said (on Feb. 17, 1950) that both pastors and laity are responsible for creating public opinion within the church. "An attitude of mute servility is as undesirable as an attitude of uncontrolled criticism."

Laypersons are to make known their needs and desires "with that freedom and confidence that befits children of God and brothers and sisters in Christ" (*LG* 37), in other words, as members of the same family. When possible, expressions of opinion about the good of the church should be made through the institutions and instruments set up for this purpose by the church, such as parish and diocesan pastoral councils, finance councils, diocesan synods, consultations, hearings, newsletters, bulletins, and web sites. Opinions could be expressed through verbal and written communications as well as through the use of other media.

Note that the right and duty to manifest one's opinions is not only "vertical," that is, to pastors and bishops, but "horizontal" as well, that is, to the rest of the faithful (c. 212.3). This kind of communication may be more difficult to achieve from a logistical standpoint, but it is equally necessary.

Indeed, the church is to be a sign to the world of that human solidarity that permits and strengthens genuine dialogue. This requires us to promote mutual esteem, respect, and harmony within the church while at the same time acknowledging legitimate diversity in order to establish ever more fruitful exchange among all who make up the one people of God, both pastors and faithful (*GS* 92).

ILLUSTRATION

The closure or merger of parishes is an event that often occasions the expression of strong feelings, with passions running high. The diocese of Pittsburgh closed or merged over one hundred parishes within a period of a very few years, with relatively little upset, protest, or appeal to higher authority, simply because the leaders took care to explain the individual situations to the people and to empower the laity in each parish to participate in the decision-making process. The diocesan officials were open and candid in their communications. They listened carefully to the voices and views of the affected laypeople, and the people responded in a positive way. The necessary reorganization took place with a minimum of painful disruption in large part because the right of all to express their needs and desires was honored.

Comment

Bishops and pastors are sometimes accused of "not listening" because they can't be reached by telephone and don't respond to letters or e-mail. But in times of crisis it may be impossible for them to handle the volume of communications. On the other hand, bishops have been literally "shouted down" while trying to listen to opinions or explain situations in local churches. Communication sometimes breaks down despite the best efforts of those involved.

In the Pittsburgh situation, special planning meetings were held wherein the chosen representatives of the parishes could share their views and needs. For normal consultations and decisions, the established channels of communications, such as parish councils, committees, bulletins, and mailings, should suffice for a healthy expression of opinions.

Is the right or freedom of expression in the church an absolute right? No, this right is limited in its exercise, as it is in other societies or organizations. In other words, just as no one has the right to cry "Fire!" in a crowded theater, so no one in the church should defame another's reputation or disregard the solemn teachings of the church. (The limitations on freedom of expression spelled out in canon 212 are listed on page 35.)

The ability to express one's needs and views is a vital part of belonging. If the faithful are full participants in the life of the church, as we claim, then all must have a say.

E. THE RIGHT TO BE INFORMED
ABOUT THE LIFE AND ACTIVITIES OF THE CHURCH

Explanation

The right to information is not one of those explicitly recognized in the Code of Canon Law, but it exists nevertheless. The right to be informed about the activities and condition of the church flows directly from the active participation of the faithful in the life of the church. The right and duty of active involvement (as stated above, the second of the rights in this category) belongs to every one of the faithful based on each person's full incorporation into the church, reception of the sacraments of initiation, and possession of the Holy Spirit. Those who are in full communion share in Christ's priestly, prophetic, and royal functions (c. 204.1), that is, in the sanctifying, teaching/learning, and pastoral roles of the church that carries on Christ's mission.

In order to exercise this right to active engagement, people must be adequately informed, especially about their own parish.

Some of the other rights of the faithful that are expressly stated in the Code cannot be exercised unless people are duly informed. The rights presuppose the knowledge of pertinent facts. For example, the freedom to make known to church leaders your needs and desires (c. 212.2) assumes that you know what the local church is doing, what it can do, and what it is not able to do. The right and duty to manifest your opinions about matters concerning the welfare of the church to the pastors and to the rest of the faithful (c. 212.3) means that you must first be knowledgeable about the church's situation. What can this parish afford? Is it growing or declining? Are the buildings in good repair or do they need maintenance? Is the evangelization program working?

Laity and ordained ministers are to communicate with and assist one another as children of God, sisters and brothers in Christ. Laypersons are to make their views known "with respect for the truth, with courage and with prudence, and in a spirit of reverence and love." Bishops and priests are to "acknowledge and promote the dignity and responsibility of the laity in the church; they should willingly make use of their prudent counsel" (*LG* 37). Such interaction can take place only in a context of trust and openness.

Access to information is essential for this level of Christian collaboration. The right of the people to information is beyond dispute. Sometimes the extent and limits of the information are at issue. No parish keeps the Mass schedule a secret, but it may not always be easy to obtain a full and up-to-date financial accounting, even though the canons call for administrators of church property to give an accounting to the faithful of the offerings that people make to the church (c. 1287.2).

The extent and degree of detail of information conveyed depends to some extent on the roles and responsibilities of the persons seeking it. For example, the members of the parish finance council (c. 537) have need for greater detail regarding fiscal data than do the rest of the parishioners. Those on the education committee must be more fully informed about the school programs and personnel than other members of the parish.

There are obvious areas of church life where confidentiality must be observed. For instance, sacramental confession, pastoral counseling, student discipline, and personnel evaluation each have an appropriate level of confidentiality. (The alleged cover-ups of clerical sexual abuse of minors revealed in 2002 showed that exaggerated confidentiality can permit misconduct to continue.) The church's life should be characterized by a presumption of openness and transparency.

CASE

In 1993 the Archdiocese of San Francisco embarked on a program of comprehensive pastoral planning. In making decisions the Planning Commission relied on parish self-studies submitted two years earlier and a series of cluster and town hall meetings held all over the city. The commission's recommendations to reorganize the parish structures within the city of San Francisco were announced in November, and the archbishop issued decrees in December to carry out those recommendations.

Among the several parishes to be suppressed was St. Brigid's. This parish was 130 years old, and although it had once had 3,500 members, it still had about 1,000 people—many of whom were highly educated and relatively affluent—attending Mass every Sunday.

The large and handsome church was constructed of un-reinforced masonry. While the structure had survived two earthquakes, it was alleged that it would cost five million dollars to retrofit the building to bring it into compliance with the city's earthquake hazard reduction statute. The parishioners appealed the decision to close the parish to the archbishop, then to the Congregation for the Clergy in Rome, and then to the Apostolic Signatura, the church's highest judicial court. All appeals were rejected; the parish was closed in 1994.

Lack of adequate and timely information was one of the principal grounds for the parishioners' appeals. No one was told that the planning process might result in parish closings; all the talk was of greater collaboration and more effective ministry. The data in the parish's own self-study was several years out of date. The elderly and ailing pastor had not adequately represented the parish during the consultation process; only once was he able to make a presentation to the commission, and there was no hint that St. Brigid's was not viable or might be closed. When the fateful recommendation was announced, the parishes affected were given two days within which to challenge it, but the pastor failed to take that opportunity and did not tell anyone else about it.

St. Brigid's parishioners were thunderstruck when news of the decision to suppress the parish was announced to them. They were completely unaware of the possibility that the parish might be closed. They promptly organized a "Save St. Brigid's" committee, and its able lawyers and engineers composed eloquent briefs challenging all aspects of the faulty information on which the decision was based. All to no avail. It was too late.

Comment

The case indicates that the parishioners' right to information was short-circuited in the planning/closing process.

Good communications are vital to the life and healthy functioning of any community, and the church is no exception. On such matters as pastoral planning, accurate and timely information can be a matter of life and death for a parish. Both pastors and parishioners have the right to know what is going on, and to have ample opportunity to present their case in any decision-making process. However, they also have the duty to remain alert and forthcoming during the process, even when the timing may be inconvenient.

F. THE RIGHT TO BE CONSULTED ON THE SELECTION OF PASTORAL LEADERS

Explanation

The right to have some voice in the selection of church leaders is one that is more implied and encouraged than explicitly acknowledged. Here we refer to several levels of leadership and several modes of selection or recruitment. In other words, the processes for the selection of a bishop, the appointment of a pastor, and the employment of a director of religious education are quite different, but the faithful should have a role in each one.

This right, like many others, is rooted in the reality of full and active membership in the church. Those fully incorporated into the church through the sacraments of initiation share in the threefold mission of teaching, sanctifying, and governing, and they are gifted by the Holy Spirit. This means that they should have a voice in choosing who their pastoral leaders will be. This does not imply the power to vote for their leaders, as in a civil election, although it does not preclude that either.

The right of consultation, like many others, should be viewed as a right of the church community, parish, or diocese, even more than an individual prerogative. That is to say, the community is the embodiment of the local church, and as such should have some say in obtaining the kind of ministerial leadership that it requires.

The practice of consultation in the selection of church leaders is very ancient. The Acts of the Apostles tells of one process in the selection of Mathias to take the place of Judas (1:15–26), and another for the choice of the seven "reputable men, filled with the Spirit and wisdom" to serve at table (6:1–6). For most of the church's history priests and people participated in the selection of their bishops by various means of consultation or subsequent approval. The public assent signified by applause during the ordination ceremony is a remnant of this earlier consultation process.

Now, when a diocesan bishop is to be named, the pope's delegate in the country asks at least some of the priests and laypersons of the diocese for their opinions, but individually and in secret (c. 377.3). (Since this entire process is shrouded in secrecy, it is impossible to know how many persons are actually consulted.) Similarly, when a pastor is appointed to a parish, the bishop must consult the dean of the deanery and usually hears from some of the priests and laypersons (c. 524). When pastoral ministers, like directors of religious education or youth ministers, are selected to serve in a parish, sometimes the pastor makes the choice himself, and sometimes there is a more participative search and selection process in which a lay committee takes the lead.

ILLUSTRATION

In the archdiocese of Washington during the 1990s, when a parish anticipated a change of pastors, there was a careful process of consultation that preceded the selection and appointment of a new pastor. The director of priest personnel would visit the parish and interview each member of the staff and the chairpersons of the parish council and the finance council. These conversations often revealed the real issues that the parish was facing. The director reviewed the history of the parish as well as the statistical reports submitted over the years.

An open meeting of parishioners was held at the parish. The regional bishop, the personnel director, and another member of the personnel board attended. The meetings were open-ended and provided ample opportunity for parishioners to comment on the state of their church and the kind of leadership they would welcome. These evening sessions were often very large and animated gatherings of the parish community.

Then the director would take his notes from all of the above sources and write a twenty- to thirty-page report on the parish and its needs. The personnel board, which consisted of five priests elected by the priests of the archdiocese, three auxiliary bishops, the archbishop, and the director, would study the report and try to match the needs of the parish with the priests available.

The board would then present the archbishop with a slate of three priests, in priority order, for the pastorate of the parish. The archbishop usually took the board's first recommended candidate, and the director would go out and interview that priest about his personal situation, his present parochial status (e.g., to determine if he was in the midst of a renewal program, a fund drive, or a construction project), and his "fit" with the prospective parish. It was a process of honest consultation, and it worked well.

Comment

The right to be consulted in the selection of church leaders is a real one, but at the present time it is difficult to exercise. The opportunities are rare, and ought to be expanded. Everyone in the church, especially the laity, should press for greater voice in the selection procedures. The logistics of effective consultation are not simple, but we could do much better than we are doing, as the Washington example demonstrates.

Secrecy inhibits thorough consultation in the selection of bishops. The recent sex abuse scandal exposed the weaknesses of the selection process. One bishop who had been accused of sexually abusing a minor was appointed to replace another bishop who was removed for the same reason; the fact that the replacement bishop had been accused was kept secret by an out-of-court settlement, and not even the papal delegate was aware of it.

When it comes to parish pastors, the current shortage of priests has made consultation of the laity into a nearly meaningless exercise in some places. The lack of priest candidates for pastorates severely limits the choices. Parishes led by lay pastoral administrators sometimes offer more opportunities for genuine consultation of the laity.

G. THE RIGHT TO ONE'S GOOD NAME

Explanation

The church affirms the right of each baptized person to a good name; it is one facet of the respect due to the human person. The human person is superior to everything else on this earth, and personal rights and duties are universal and inviolable (GS 26).

In its canonical list of the rights and obligations of all the Christian faithful, the church states the rule as a negative prohibition: no one is permitted to harm illegitimately the good reputation that a person possesses (c. 220). In a community whose highest law is that of love, it might seem that concern for a Christian brother's or sister's good reputation could be taken for granted. But we are also sinful people, hence the law.

A person's good name or the public esteem that one enjoys is a precious possession; St. Thomas Aquinas called it the most precious of our temporal goods, more valuable than wealth, and for that reason he judged that detraction is worse than theft (*Summa Theologiae*, II-II, 73, 3). As precious as it is, a reputation can be damaged or lost by someone's careless remark, malicious gossip, or false accusation. Because the personal harm can be so great, detraction and calumny are punishable offences in the church's criminal law (c. 1390.2–3).

There are times when revelation of someone's wrongdoing or criminal activity is legitimate and even necessary, such as when one is called to testify in a criminal trial or obliged to reveal an impediment to a forthcoming marriage (c. 1069).

CASE

The issue of damaged reputations was a prominent feature of the scandalous revelations in 2002 of clerical sexual abuse of minors in the United States. Both accused priests and alleged victims suffered grave, sometimes irreparable, harm to their good names.

A young priest in a diocese in the southeastern United States was accused of having kissed and fondled a seventeen-year-old girl when she was a willing guest at his summer cottage. This occurred a few times during the year 1977. Several years later the young woman complained to the archbishop about the sexual contact between her and the priest. The priest admitted what he had done, and apologized for it. He received counseling and therapy at a sex abuse treatment center, and, at the completion of sessions, he was judged to be at low risk of repeat offense. Subsequently he was appointed and reappointed to pastorates; he was well loved by his parishioners and his evaluations were exemplary.

In 2002 the archbishop, under directions from the Congregation for the Doctrine of the Faith, changed the archdiocesan policies so that "any priest against whom credible allegations of sexual abuse of minors are made will no longer be able to continue in ministry of any kind." The archbishop's advisory panel reviewed the files of those previously accused. Although the events were now twenty-five years in the past and there had been no allegations of any subsequent abuses, the priest was put on administrative leave from his parish ministry. The archdiocese issued a press release saying that the reason for his leave was for a review of an allegation of sexual abuse of a minor in 1977. It spoke of his therapy and of the earlier decision to allow him to continue in ministry.

The priest felt that his reputation was permanently damaged and that his life was in ruins. He became despondent and died within a month.

Comment

When a minor is sexually abused by a priest, even when the minor is a fully consenting participant, the physical, psychological, and spiritual damage to the abused child or youth can be and often is enormous. The real harm that has been done far outweighs the loss of good name of the victim or of the perpetrator. (Obviously each case must be judged on its own merits.) However, a good reputation is a precious possession, and the public disclosure of past failings endangers the reputations of both parties.

H. THE RIGHT TO PROTECT ONE'S PRIVACY

Explanation

The church recognizes the personal right to privacy both in its teachings and in its rules of discipline. The Second Vatican Council's *Pasotral Constitution on the Church in the Modern World* (*Gaudium et Spes*) acknowledges the right of every person to the protection of his or her private life as one facet of the sublime dignity of the human person (*GS* 26). The Code of Canon Law states the right in the context of a negative prohibition: no one is permitted to injure the right of any person to protect her or his own privacy (c. 220). Here, our context is not simply the human family, but the community of the faithful; the right to privacy exists even within the relatively intimate community of faith, hope, and love. We are sisters and brothers in Christ, but we still have our need for and right to an appropriate privacy.

The privacy concerns in the church focus on moral and personal issues, especially matters of conscience. The forum of conscience is inviolable; no one can oblige another to reveal his or her conscience.

This arena of conscience enjoys many protections in the church's rules: the absolute confidentiality of the seal of confession (c. 983), the prohibition against use of knowledge learned in confession (c. 984), the freedom to choose confessors (c. 991), the law against confessors or spiritual directors having any part in admitting or dismissing seminarians (c. 240.2), the limits on investigating candidates for religious life (c. 642), the law against religious superiors inducing their subjects to manifest their consciences to them (c. 630.5), and the exemption from testifying to matters held under professional secrecy or those which might bring harm to witnesses or their families (c. 1548.2).

Besides the "forum of conscience," other privacy concerns extend to one's physical person, communications of various kinds, financial, medical, and criminal records, psychological assessments, and the confidentiality of all of these records. These issues arise in relationship to candidates for holy orders, religious life, or church employment, those in substance abuse therapy, those accused of sexual abuse who are in evaluation or therapy, even those wishing to marry or requesting a declaration of the nullity of their marriage.

Instances like these present situations that test the limits of an individual's personal right to privacy on the one hand and the common good of church communities and the protection of their members on the other. In other words, there are certain things, normally within the zone of personal privacy, that the church has a right to know. Conversely, there may be times when the church's claim to need to know unjustly intrudes on personal privacy.

ILLUSTRATION

One western diocese, in an attempt to supervise and give support to priests who were found to have abused minors or had other serious problems such as addictive substance abuse, gambling, or sexual activity with adults, enacted a policy of intrusive inspections of the priests' residences. The policy called for unscheduled visits to the clerics' homes at any time of the day or night, seven days a week. Other possible restrictions included limits on the priests' computer use, monitoring of their travel, and relocation of their residences.

Most priests who are in a rebound and recovery mode, the bishop said, are grateful for some follow-up and fraternal support. This policy was an attempt to formalize that support.

The announcement of the new policy was greeted by a firestorm of negative reaction from the priests of the diocese. They reacted both against the threatened intrusions into their personal privacy and to the fact that the priests had not been consulted in the process of developing the policy. The bishop saw the point of the priests' protests and, after promptly suspending enforcement of the new policy, submitted it for review by the priests' senate.

Comment

Personnel files in parish and diocesan offices and the headquarters of religious communities of men and women contain many records that demand confidentiality in the interests of the privacy of individuals. The files may include police background checks for criminal activity, tests for use of drugs or other controlled substances, psychological evaluations, medical tests for venereal diseases or HIV/AIDS, court testimony about abusive marriages, illegitimacy, and more.

Access to such files is strictly limited and their confidentiality is guarded. But over time the personnel who have supervision over and access to these files change, and the danger of accidental revelations or indiscreet uses of personal information increases. The church attempts to safeguard the confidentiality of these records. The rules for preservation, access, and security of diocesan archives serve as a paradigm (cc. 486–490).

2. RIGHTS TO WORD, SACRAMENTS, AND PASTORAL CARE

A. THE RIGHT TO HEAR THE WORD OF GOD

Explanation

The right of the faithful to hear the word of God and to be nourished by it is basic to membership in a Christian community (c. 213). God's self-revelation in Jesus Christ and Christ's message of salvation constitute our most precious heritage. The Holy Spirit makes the living voice of the gospel ring out in the church, and through it in the world, leading us into the whole truth and making the message of Christ dwell in us in all its richness (*DV* 8).

Priests have a solemn duty to proclaim the gospel and to explain it so thatthe faithful can apply it to their own lives (c. 757). Preaching is the principal way that this obligation is carried out, especially in the homily at Mass, but the gospel is proclaimed by word and witness in many other ways as well. Indeed, deacons, religious men and women, and laypersons are called upon to cooperate in the ministry of the word (cc. 757–759). Bishops are the moderators of the entire ministry of the word within the dioceses entrusted to them (cc. 756.2, 386).

Proclamation of the gospel is the church's primary and foremost ministry.

These manifold responsibilities are in response to the fundamental right of the people of God to have full and fruitful access to God's holy word. It is to be provided to them completely and faithfully, by every means possible, and in ways accommodated to their abilities to understand (cc. 760, 761, 769). The word must also be proclaimed to those of the faithful who do not have access to ordinary pastoral care, such as military personnel, shut-ins, exiles, travelers, and prisoners (c. 771.1).

CASE

Father Kelly is the beloved pastor of St. Joseph's parish, where he has served for more than twenty years. His preaching, however, leaves something to be desired. He always gives a homily at Mass, but he spends little or no time preparing it. As a result, his homilies are very repetitious. Moreover, Father Kelly never fails to mention the evil of abortion and the right to life. Most of the parishioners look forward to the preaching of the director of religious education. She has a degree in theology, studied homiletics, and is an excellent preacher. Father Kelly has her preach at least once every month (although not in place of the homily).

One of the reasons why St. Joseph's parishioners cherish Father Kelly is that he is devoted to those who are sick in the hospital, or confined to their own homes or to one of the three nursing homes in the parish. He visits them regularly, brings them Holy Communion, hears their confessions and anoints them when appropriate, and always leaves them a large-print brochure with Sunday's biblical readings along with some points for reflection.

Comment

Father Kelly is to be commended for his pastoral care for the sick and home-bound members of the parish. His concern to see that they too are nourished by God's word as well as by the sacraments is exemplary. However, by not preparing his own homilies he is not being fair to the ordinary Mass-going parishioners. Good preaching is hard work, and time and energy given to its preparation are essential to its effectiveness. The people have a right to hear the full range of God's message of salvation, and not to be subjected to the repetition of a few themes, even one as important as the right to life.

Father Kelly would be well advised to enlist the assistance of some of the parishioners in evaluating and planning his homilies as well as the preaching of the DRE.

B. THE RIGHT TO RECEIVE THE SACRAMENTS

Explanation

The faithful have a right to receive the assistance they need from the spiritual goods of the church; in particular they have the right to receive the sacraments (c. 213). The church's ministers are forbidden to deny the sacraments to those who seek them at appropriate times, are properly disposed, and are not prohibited by law from receiving them (c. 843.1). The sacraments are actions of Christ and the church, signs that express and strengthen faith, render worship to God, sanctify God's people by the power of the Holy Spirit, and show forth the church's communion (c. 840).

Because the sacraments are of central importance in life of the Catholic Church, the church's rules try to assure in many ways that its people have ready access to them. These rules reinforce the people's right to the sacraments.

Baptism, of course, is the gateway to all the other sacraments; only those who have been baptized can receive the other sacraments (c. 842.1). Baptism frees us from sin, makes us children of God, configures us to Christ, and incorporates us into the church (c. 849). Confirmation strengthens the baptized, enriches them with the gift of the Holy Spirit and ties them closer to the church (c. 879). The proper sequence of the sacraments for full Christian initiation is baptism, confirmation, and Eucharist (c. 842.2).

The Eucharist is the summit and source of all worship and Christian life (see *LG* 11, *SC* 10). Christ himself is contained, offered, and received in the sacrament of the Eucharist. It unifies the people of God, and builds up the body of Christ; all the other sacraments are ordered to it (c. 897). Any baptized person can and must be admitted to Holy Communion, unless he or she is prohibited by law (c. 912). Participation at the table of the Eucharist is the primary and ultimate sign of being in full communion with the church. It is a fundamental right of all Catholic Christians.

Pastors are to see to it that the Eucharist is the center of the parish assembly of the faithful, and are to urge parishioners to take an active part in its celebration and to receive Holy Communion frequently (cc. 528.2, 898). The faithful may celebrate the Eucharist and receive Holy Communion in any Catholic rite (c. 923).

In the sacrament of penance the faithful obtain forgiveness from God for the sins they have committed since baptism, and they are reconciled to the church (c. 959). The faithful are free to confess to any confessor of their choice, even one of another rite (c. 991). Those having the care of souls (pastors, associates, chaplains) are obliged to see to it that confessions are heard when reasonably requested as well as at scheduled times (c. 986.1).

In the anointing of the sick, the church commends those who are seriously ill to the Lord so that he might relieve and save them (c. 998). Pastors of souls as well as caregivers are to see to it that the sick are anointed at an appropriate time (c. 1001). Those having care of souls are to be vigilant that the faithful who are in danger of death are nourished by Holy Communion in the form of Viaticum while fully conscious (cc. 921, 922).

CASE

In the hard-fought campaign for the presidency of the United States in 2004, one of the candidates was a Catholic who had a legislative voting record that was "pro-choice" on the issue of abortion. Several bishops issued statements that such a Catholic politician should be denied Holy Communion, on the grounds that his votes constituted formal cooperation in the evil of abortion, gave scandal to the Catholic faithful, and meant the he "obstinately persisted in manifest grave sin," one of the grounds for exclusion from eucharistic communion (c. 915).

Other bishops cautioned against interpreting a politician's votes in the hurly-burly of the law-making process as implying a state of personal sin. They pointed out that the cooperation represented by a vote in the legislature can be viewed as quite remote from the actual procurement of abortions, adding that the element of real scandal is not easy to discern in the context of prudential judgments on public policy within a pluralistic society. Further, they noted that there is a long-standing practice in the church not to make a public judgment about the state of soul of those who present themselves for Holy Communion.

The numerous public statements and the furor generated by this debate became a major feature of the political campaign.

When the American bishops met in June 2004 to deliberate the issue among themselves, they discussed it for several hours over a period of three days and resolved (by a vote of 183 to 6) that the decision to deny Communion rests "with the individual bishop in accord with the established canonical and pastoral principles. Bishops can legitimately make different judgments on the most prudent course of pastoral action."

The bishops continued to speak with diverse voices. The Catholic presidential candidate lost the election by a very narrow margin.

Comment

The sacraments are sacred symbols right at the heart of Catholic life and worship. From time to time access to the sacraments becomes entangled with moral judgments, like the status of divorced and remarried couples or the sale of contraceptives by Catholic pharmacists. The issue of access to the sacraments can also get mixed up in political controversies, like the criminalization of abortion or military service in an unjust war. For the most part, however, the Catholic Church has left the judgment of worthiness for the sacraments to the consciences of the faithful.

C. THE RIGHT TO PASTORAL CARE

Explanation

The rights of every Catholic to hear the word of God and to receive the sacraments have already been explained. These are two aspects—the central and most vital elements—of what is more broadly described as pastoral care. But pastoral care includes other areas of ministry and assistance besides these two, and all the baptized faithful also have a right to pastoral care in this larger sense.

The specific elements of pastoral care are spelled out in the responsibilities of the church's ministers, especially those of pastors of parishes and bishops of dioceses. These duties reflect the specifics of the right of the faithful to pastoral care.

A parish pastor, assisted by other priests, deacons, and laypersons, is charged with the pastoral care of Christian faithful who make up the parish community (c. 515). This pastoral care is described in terms of the traditional threefold functions of teaching, sanctifying, and governing (c. 519; PO 4–9). These functions are explained in some detail:

- Teaching includes proclaiming the word of God not only in homilies and catechetics, instruction, and education, but also in counseling, works of social justice, and the evangelization of those in the parish who don't practice their religion or don't profess the true faith (cc. 528.1, 773, 776–777).

- Sanctifying means the devout celebration of Mass and the other sacraments, with the active participation of the faithful, but it also means the encouragement of family prayer, helping spouses and parents to carry out their family responsibilities, caring for the sick and dying, reaching out to assist the poor, the afflicted, the lonely, exiles, and those especially burdened (cc. 528.2, 529.1).

- Governing first of all means knowing the parishioners entrusted to the pastor, visiting their families, and sharing their cares and anxieties. It also includes the administration of the parish and its buildings and properties, cooperating with the pastoral and financial councils, promoting the roles of the laity in the church's mission, fostering parish organizations, helping parishioners collaborate with the diocesan church, and maintaining parish records (cc. 529, 532, 535–537).

Bishops of dioceses are also to carry out these same functions of teaching, sanctifying, and governing, in the dioceses entrusted to them, with the cooperation of the priests, deacons, and laity (c. 375; *CD* 11–18):

- Teaching implies not only preaching and giving instruction personally, but seeing that the ministry of the word, catechetics, and education are organized and promoted throughout the diocese (c. 386).

- Sanctifying calls for the bishop to preside regularly at the Eucharist himself, to show a personal example of holiness in charity, humility, and simplicity of life, to endeavor to have the faithful entrusted to him grow in grace through the celebration of the sacraments, and to promote the holiness of the people in their own ways of life (c. 387).

- Governing for a bishop means first of all being solicitous for all the faithful entrusted to him and acting with charity toward all those not in full communion with the church. A diocesan bishop has legislative, executive, and judicial powers, often exercised by his appointed assistants. He is charged with maintaining the church's discipline in the diocese, exercising vigilance over the administration of church property, collaborating with the pastoral, presbyteral, and finance councils, overseeing the parishes and institutions of the diocese, fostering the various forms of the apostolate, and encouraging and coordinating the works of the laity in the different areas of the diocese (cc. 391–396).

This overview of the responsibilities of pastors and bishops outlines, at least in broad strokes, the right of the people of the church to pastoral care. The right does not imply that the faithful are entitled to be passive recipients, like guests at a banquet, of the care provided by others, their ministers. Rather, the right points to some aspects of pastoral care that are needed, expected, and ought to be provided within the local Christian community, most often through the collaboration of its members, lay volunteers, professional staff, and ordained ministers.

CASE

Father Angelo had been the pastor of St. Jerome's for ten years when Bishop Murphy asked him to move to another parish. Father Angelo hadn't been an ideal pastor; parish income hadn't kept up with inflation, the school had to be closed, and the other buildings weren't very well maintained. But Father Angelo was a "people person"; he knew his people and related well to them. He trusted the laity, supported most of their initiatives, and promoted good liturgical celebrations. He worked closely with the elected parish council, and the council became the effective leadership group in the parish.

Bishop Murphy assigned Father Kurt to St. Jerome's, even though some people had complained about his rather autocratic style at his last two assignments. The bishop did not have many choices, and he knew that the finances and physical plant at St. Jerome's both needed improvement. He urged Father Kurt to work collaboratively with the people as Father Angelo had.

Father Kurt was young and vigorous. He said his prayers dutifully and played by the rules. He also preached and celebrated Mass well. Shortly after he arrived, Father Kurt fired the janitor and housekeeper and hired new ones. He could not account for all the keys to parish buildings, so he had all of the locks changed. After completing an assessment of needed repairs, he began talking to people about the money to pay for these repairs. He met with the parish council and laid out his plans. The council responded by proposing a plan of its own. Father Kurt gradually stopped consulting the council, cancelled some of its meetings, and postponed the election of new members.

Father Kurt sought to economize by not replacing the coordinator of liturgy when she resigned, and by cutting the music budget in half. He cancelled the free coffee and rolls after the Sunday Masses. As the eucharistic liturgies became less participative and more perfunctory, parishioners began to look around for better celebrations elsewhere. Father Kurt insisted to his own people and to the neighboring pastors that parish boundaries had to be observed so that pastoral care could be provided to the people in an orderly way. Sunday Mass attendance at St. Jerome's began to decline, although the collections actually increased due to the tithing program that Kurt introduced.

Comment

Who is the better pastor, Father Angelo or Father Kurt? Which one is more likely to provide good pastoral care at St. Jerome's in the long run?

The case hints at the radically diverse approaches to pastoral care in the Catholic Church. The provision of pastoral care is a limitless task, and there are many ways and means of accomplishing it. But providing pastoral care is not solely the responsibility of the parish pastor. At its best, provision of pastoral care results from the harmonious collaboration of many people who love and work for their community.

D. THE RIGHT TO ONE'S OWN SPIRITUAL LIFE

Explanation

The right to religious freedom is firmly based on the dignity of the human person (*DH* 2). This right implies both immunity from coercion in religious matters and the freedom to act in accord with one's conscience, individually or in association with others.

The practice of religion consists principally of acts that are voluntary and free, in which one relates oneself to God directly. Our social nature requires that these interior religious acts be expressed externally; we share our faith and witness to our religion communally as well as personally (*DH* 3). This basic human right is honored within the church, as well as in most civil societies.

God calls each of us to serve him in spirit and in truth, by personal choice. We must never lose sight of the Catholic teaching that our response to God in faith is a free act; the act of faith is by its very nature voluntary (*DH* 10). The church is a community of those who have freely chosen Christ as their truth, and we witness to that truth in freedom, both personally and corporately.

The church acknowledges this fundamental right of religious freedom in many ways, but three are especially recognized in its canonical regulations:

1. Freedom of conscience

All persons are obliged to seek the truth about God and his church, and to embrace and observe that truth when they discover it (c. 748). The law we have from God is the one inscribed in our hearts (Rom 2:15), its observance is our dignity, and our consciences bear witness to it. Conscience is the most intimate center and sanctuary of a person in which the voice of God echoes (*GS* 16, 26). We must faithfully form and then follow our consciences. (The right to form and follow one's conscience is more fully explored below in the section on rights to formation.)

2. Freedom to worship according to one's own rite

The various ritual traditions manifest the rich diversity within the church. There are twenty-two distinct rites within the one communion of the Catholic Church. The Latin rite is the largest of them. Other rites include the Ukrainian, Maronite, Ruthenian, Melkite, and Romanian.

"Rite" signifies much more than distinctive liturgical ceremonies or rituals. It also means a theological, spiritual, cultural, and disciplinary heritage manifested in a church united by its own hierarchy. All Catholics have the right to worship according to their own rite (c. 214). In practice, the exercise of this right is sometimes rendered difficult due to the dispersion of the people and the paucity of their priests. Still, the church strives to preserve and protect these distinct rites and to facilitate the people's access to them.

3. Freedom to follow one's form of spiritual life

The faithful have the right to follow their own form of spiritual life so long as it is consonant with the teaching of the church (c. 214). The many spiritual traditions also manifest the wondrous diversity within the communion of the church. People are free to follow the prompting of the Holy Spirit in pursuing the practice and growth of their Christian lives.

Some schools of spirituality sprang out of the church's great religious movements: monastic, contemplative, mendicant, missionary, and apostolic. They inspired such traditions as the Benedictine, Franciscan, Carmelite, and Ignatian. Other spiritualities focus on specific features of the faith, like the Blessed Sacrament, Divine Mercy, the gifts of the Holy Spirit, charity, the Blessed Mother, the divine office, or devotion to a particular saint. The rich variety of these spiritualities is one of the glories of the church. Here again, however, the public and communal practice of these various forms of spiritual life is sometimes hampered by the lack of ministerial leadership or by the competing demands for time and space within a given parish.

CASE

Emil Nagy had been an All Saints parishioner for many years, and Father O'Connor thought that he knew him pretty well. But he was flabbergasted when Emil came to ask his pastor if he could start a Christian–Zen Buddhist meditation group in the parish. "Emil," the priest exclaimed, "are you leaving the church or have you taken leave of your senses? We're Christians here at All Saints!"

Emil patiently explained to Father O'Connor that he had been quietly pursuing Zen Buddhism for several years, along with a small group of friends. He felt stronger than ever in his Catholic faith. He asked his pastor if he had noticed that both his financial contributions and his singing in the parish choir had both improved in recent years. Emil went on to say that he had arrived at a richer appreciation for his faith and a new sense of peace and wholeness from his practice of Zen meditation. He found no contradictions or even tensions between the Catholic tradition and the way of Zen.

Father O'Connor said that they had all sorts of devotions and study groups in the parish already, and couldn't he please just join one of those? "Why can't you practice your meditation during our adoration of the Blessed Sacrament?" he asked.

Emil answered that he was already doing this, but he added that his group needed opportunities to meet, learn, converse, and reflect together. The group had outgrown their family rooms and needed more space.

Father O'Connor responded that there were already so many different groups in the parish that it would not be possible to find time in church or space in the activities center for them to pray or meet.

Emil smiled, gave Father a book on Buddhist and Christian practice, and said he'd come back to see him in a month. As a parting shot Father O'Connor asked, "Do you expect me to advertise Buddhism in the parish bulletin? Do you know what the bishop would do to me if he heard about that?"

"Don't worry, Father," Emil replied, "I'll go and tell him that Buddhism has made me a better Christian. It has brought me closer to Jesus."

Comment

Parishes, especially large and multi-ethnic ones, sometimes have to do balancing acts in their attempt to meet people's requests for different devotions and spiritual practices. Accommodating them requires agility and diplomacy, but it is well worth the effort. Even more than a matter of people's freedom and rights in the church, these multiple spiritualities are manifestations of the Holy Spirit, and a testimony to the kaleidoscopic diversity within the Catholic tradition.

E. THE RIGHT TO A CATHOLIC FUNERAL

Explanation

Deceased members of the Christian faithful must be given ecclesiastical funerals (c. 1176.1). This obligation of pastors reflects the right to Christian burial on the part of church members.

The church shows reverence for the physical body as an integral part of the human person. The body is a full partner with the soul on the path toward salvation, and it is destined to share in the resurrection and everlasting life. The church's funeral rites honor the bodies of the faithful, seek spiritual support for the deceased, and try to bring the solace of hope to those who remain alive. The church recommends burial of bodies, but does not prohibit their cremation (c. 1176.2–3).

There are three circumstances in which this right to a church funeral is not honored (c. 1184):

1. when persons formally and publicly separated themselves from the church (apostates, heretics, or schis-

matics; these technical categories are defined in canon 751; the rule does not imply that those who have simply ceased practicing their faith are to be deprived of funerals),

2. when persons chose to have their bodies cremated for reasons contrary to the faith, or

3. when the persons were manifest sinners who cannot be given funerals without public scandal to the faithful. (Persons in irregular marriage situations or those who committed suicide are not usually considered to be in the category of manifest sinners.)

If in any of these three situations the persons gave some sign of repentance, then they are to be given a funeral in the church. When there is some doubt in any of these cases, then the bishop or his delegate is to be consulted.

CASE

John, a Catholic and a prominent businessman in the city, died suddenly at age thirty-one. His parents arranged for his funeral at the largest church in the city. When the bishop learned that John's business enterprise was a gay bar and dance club, he issued a statement forbidding John's funeral to be held in any church in the diocese. John's parents were hurt and offended by the bishop's ruling, and they arranged to have John buried from an Episcopal church.

Three days later the bishop sent John's mother a letter stating that he regretted his hasty decision and the fact that it had resulted in what was perceived as John's unjust condemnation. He said that he would preside at a Mass for the family, in memory of John, in the original church.

Comment

The bishop was justified in intervening in this pastoral decision to bury from the church a person whose well-known business was morally questionable. He initially concluded that what went on at the club was inconsistent with Catholic moral teaching. However, the bishop reconsidered his first judgment because of the harm that it had caused to John's reputation, and possibly he re-evaluated the nature of John's enterprise or the extent of John's personal responsibility for some of the activities there.

Sometimes such pastoral decisions are very difficult, and involve balancing the right to a church burial against the scandal that could be caused by providing a church funeral for a person with an extremely bad reputation, such as someone known for engaging in gang violence, or drug trafficking, or human exploitation. The extent of public scandal is not easy to predict. It is often possible for the church's ministers to draw attention to God's merciful forgiveness and the needs of a grieving family while at the same time avoiding undue ostentation and publicity. For example, Frank Sinatra's funeral (Los Angeles, 1998) was celebrated in the cathedral by the archbishop, but it was closed to all media and photographers, as well as to the general public.

3. RIGHTS TO INITIATIVES AND ACTIVITIES

A. THE RIGHT TO INITIATE, PROMOTE, AND SUSTAIN APOSTOLIC ACTIVITIES

Explanation

The church affirms the right of every Catholic to initiate, promote, and sustain apostolic actions. The faithful hold this right precisely because they actively participate in the mission of the church (c. 216).

What is meant by "apostolic action"? The expression is Catholic shorthand for carrying on the work of Christ and of the Holy Spirit. "The apostolate . . . is primarily directed to making the message of Christ clear to the world by word and deed and to sharing his grace" (*AA* 6). It begins with the witness of a Christian life, proceeds to the proclamation of Christ, centers on the transformation of the temporal order, and never neglects works of charity (*AA* 6–8).

What is new here? Sharing in the mission of the church as it carries on the work of Christ has been a right and duty of the baptized since the very beginning. But for a very long time it was assumed that laypersons were invited and urged to participate in activities that were initiated and promoted by the hierarchy, that is, by the pope, bishops, or priests. What is new in this statement of a right is that both the initiative and the follow-through can come from laity without prompting from the hierarchy. When it comes to apostolic actions, any member of the church can be a self-starter.

The canon adds one limiting factor to this right: no undertaking is to claim the name "Catholic" without the consent of church authority (c. 216). It is a "truth in advertising" qualification. Attaching the label "Catholic" to a project or organization can lead others to think that it has a measure of official approval. If the promoters want to have that kind of identity, they are required to ask for it.

Another cautionary note is the concern for good order in the church. Apostolic efforts should be coordinated and not competitive; duplicated and divided efforts are sometimes harmful. For example, for many years there were two very similar configurations of the Marriage Encounter movement.

The source for this canon (AA 24–25) reminds everyone that, although apostolic initiatives can be established by laypersons and regulated by their prudent judgment, the church's leadership must foster them, coordinate them, and see that they contribute to the common good of the church. This collaboration should be familial, like that between sisters and brothers.

CASE

The wife of a very successful funeral director was suddenly widowed at the age of fifty-six due to the tragic death of her husband. She had five children and several grandchildren and was a co-owner of the family business. She was also very active in her Catholic parish. She could have simply immersed herself in those family, business, and parochial concerns, but in addition to continuing those involvements, she initiated an organization to counsel the bereaved, calling upon her own experience and knowledge. The organization she founded is called "Wounded Healers," and it consists of groups of volunteers who help spouses, children, siblings, and friends work through their grieving process. There was no such organization or ministry in her area at the time she began this work. She has helped the movement spread to many parts of the United States and Canada.

Comment

In the Catholic tradition, comforting the afflicted is one of the spiritual works of mercy. In this case it is closely related to burying the dead, a corporal work of mercy.

This is a classic example of an apostolic initiative taken by one layperson, based on her own experiences, learning, and gifts. The initiative was then organized and imitated so that it has benefited thousands of people. The church is built up by such promptings of the Holy Spirit.

B. THE RIGHT TO FOUND AND DIRECT ASSOCIATIONS FOR RELIGIOUS PURPOSES

Explanation

The church acknowledges the right of members of the faithful, laypersons or ministers, to found, form, and guide associations, on their own initiative and without the prior approval of any hierarchical authority. The rule that recognizes this right (c. 215) envisions associations for charitable or religious purposes or "to promote the Christian vocation in the world." In other words, it encompasses a very wide range of faith-related organizations. After all, the work and witness of Christian men and women in their own worlds can and does take many modes and forms. The principle stated here is the freedom to join together in an organized way so that the purposes can be carried on and achieved more effectively through common effort.

The right of association is based on the social nature of all human persons, but here it is supported by the faithful

- being incorporated in Christ through baptism,

- made sharers in Christ's priestly, prophetic, and royal functions, and

- called to exercise the mission that God has entrusted the church to fulfill in the world (c. 204.1).

This right and freedom to band together for Christian purposes belongs to every one of the faithful.

The scope of the associations can be local, diocesan, national, or international. The authorization for and description of associations is set forth very well in the *Decree on the Apostolate of the Laity* from the Second Vatican Council (especially *AA* 18–20). The point of the decree was to affirm the lay initiative to associate, but not to encourage the multiplication of similar associations.

Associations of the Christian faithful can be recognized or even recommended by church authorities, but this is not required. There are degrees of this official approval, and with them come greater or lesser degrees of oversight and control (cf. cc. 298–329).

Examples of recent associations in the American church include: Voice of the Faithful, Catholics United for the Faith, Call to Action, Pax Christi, National Association of Lay Ministers, Future Church, Dignity, Separated and Divorced Catholics,

National Leadership Roundtable on Church Management, and many more.

CASE

In 1996, a small group of Catholics in Nebraska began to organize a local affiliate of Call to Action, a national lay-led organization that focuses on justice and peace. They wrote to the bishops of the three dioceses in that state of their intentions. In response, the bishop of Lincoln issued legislation that threatened excommunication for any Catholic who retained membership for more than two months in Call to Action (or in a list of other groups). He had made a judgment that membership in such associations was nearly always a danger to the member's faith.

The Call to Action members were stunned by the bishop's action, which immediately became controversial and attracted national media attention. The group had recourse, sequentially, to the bishops of the province, to the national bishops' conference, and then to Congregation of Bishops in Rome, all without result. The local group still exists. No other bishop has taken similar punitive action against Call to Action.

Comment

The laypeople in Lincoln were exercising their right to associate, and presumably they were doing so with good will and positive intent. Call to Action is viewed as liberal, progressive, and reformist.

The bishop, who has both teaching and pastoral authority, is charged to care for his people. In the past bishops have punished those who joined "an association which plots against the church" (c. 1374), such as the Communist Party in post-war

Europe. The bishop of Lincoln perceived the introduction of Call to Action into the diocese as unwelcome and possibly dangerous for the people. Yet, his severely punitive and almost unprecedented action was widely viewed as an extreme overreaction. No one has imitated it.

What should the bishop have done? Would dialogue have been successful? Could he have achieved some compromise regarding the group's statement of aims? Should he have simply left them alone?

C. THE RIGHT TO HOLD MEETINGS AND TO HOLD THEM ON CHURCH PROPERTY

Explanation

The right to call and conduct meetings is closely related to the right of association. Indeed, the two rights, although distinct, are stated in the same canon (c. 215). In civil society we are accustomed to distinguish the right of assembly from the right of association. Since gathering a group together is an overt and observable exercise of the right of association, it is sometimes meetings rather than other acts of associating—such as enrolling members or contributing money—that are resisted. It is not unusual for new or "controversial" groups to be denied permission to meet on church property.

The church clearly affirms the right of all the faithful "to hold meetings for the common pursuit of the purposes" of their associations (c. 215). The purpose for which meetings are held is related to the nature of the group. The meetings are to be in pursuit of the aims of the association, but the nature of the meetings is not further specified or limited. In other words, the kinds of gatherings can vary widely: organizational, informational, social, spiritual, or financial.

Likewise, the scope of the meetings is not limited. The canon does not apply only to local or parochial gatherings; it can apply also to meetings that are diocesan-wide, regional, national, or even international.

The source for this canon on the right to hold meetings is the Vatican II decree on the apostolate of the laity (especially AA 18–22). This section of the document focuses on various forms of concerted apostolic activity. It points out not only that human beings are social by nature, but that God has invited believers in Christ into one people of God. Their united activity is a sign of the communion and unity of the church. Christ is present in some way when they meet. "Where two or three are gathered in my name, I am there among them" (Matt 18:20).

The clearly stated right to form associations and to hold meetings in pursuit of their aims (c. 215) legitimates the gatherings wherever they are held. It does not, however, in and of itself, mean that there is a further right to hold those meetings on church property. Still, there are good reasons to infer such a right, or at least a positive presumption that those who request the use of church property for an association meeting might have the benefit of the doubt.

First, it helps to reflect on the kind of church property being requested for use. What is the nature of the facility? A parish hall where parties, wedding receptions, and funeral luncheons are held is very different from the parish church itself where Mass is celebrated and the Blessed Sacrament is reserved. A grade-school cafeteria is different from a college classroom or a university auditorium. The diocesan pastoral center might be viewed as different from a church basement or a parish activity center. What is appropriate in one space may not be appropriate in another.

Then, the nature of the group and its meetings also matters. Is it faith-based or religion-related or is it purely social or political? (Remember that in the United States churches' federal tax exempt status carries with it the obligation of neutrality regarding specific political candidates.) Is it a well-known and traditional organization or a new and "controversial" one? Are those requesting a meeting parishioners or strangers? Are they Catholics? Any or all of the foregoing may be given use of church facilities, but the decision regarding this may require more discerning judgment in some cases than in others.

The discernment, in a parish setting, may fall to the pastor, a lay minister, the parish council, or a facilities committee. Those planning a meeting and preparing to make a request for space might engage in a similar discernment.

In making such a judgment the following factors, among others, should be considered:

- the fact that each one of the faithful has an active share in the work of Christ and in the mission of the church (c. 204);

- the right of the faithful to make known their needs and desires, and to manifest their opinions to the leaders of the church and to the rest of the faithful (c. 212);

- the right of the faithful to found and direct associations and to hold meetings related to them (c. 215);

- the right of the faithful to promote and sustain apostolic activity on their own initiative (c. 216);

- the right and duty of the faithful to exercise their gifts of grace (charisms) in the church and in the world, for good of humanity and the building up of the church (AA 3);

- the duty of pastors to recognize and promote the proper role of lay members of the Christian faithful in the church's mission (c. 529.2; *PO* 9);

- the encouragement of ecumenical prayer, conversations, and cooperative efforts at the parish level (1993 *Directory on Ecumenism*);

- the participation of all of the faithful in the church's teaching function (c. 204; *LG* 12); consideration of the level of the teaching related to the group, e.g., divine mercy, civil rights, right to life (cc. 750–753);

- the fact that church property belongs to the juridic person (e.g., the parish as a legal entity) that acquired it, not to the pastor or to individual members of the parish (or even to all of them collectively), but that the parishioners do have a canonically recognized interest in the parish that makes their use of the property more than appropriate; and

- the maxim repeated by Pope John XXIII: "In essentials unity, in doubtful matters freedom, in all things charity" (see *UR* 4).

The consideration of these factors, in most instances, will incline toward a positive judgment. Generally speaking, the benefit of the doubt should be given to those asking to hold meetings on church property, but still discernment is appropriate.

As is the case with the exercise of all rights in the church, certain balancing or moderating factors are at play. They are: the common good of the church, the rights of others, and our duties toward others (c. 223.1).

It helps to have policies or guidelines in place before individual requests are made. The even-handed application of objective criteria avoids the appearance of arbitrary decisions or favoritism.

In the articulation of such parish policies on the use of facilities, one factor to ponder is the meaning or symbolism of holding meetings on church property. Does it imply endorsement, or is it simply neutral hospitality? How will it be perceived? A published policy statement can clarify the implications of hosting or simply allowing gatherings.

CASE

A local affiliate of a national organization decided to meet to protest the diocese's policy of not allowing female altar servers. In 1995 they held two meetings, with permission, in Catholic parishes. On both occasions a small group of Catholics who supported the diocesan policy disrupted the meetings by shouting, singing, shoving, and cutting microphone cords. On the second occasion the county police arrested eight of the members of the disrupting group for trespass.

A few days after that second meeting the chancellor of the diocese sent a memorandum to all of the pastors stating that "pastors and other administrators of church properties are not to allow use of their facilities to groups who advocate against church teachings or legitimate church practices."

Six of the disrupters were subsequently tried and convicted of trespass in civil court. At their trial they testified that they had notified the chancellor of the diocese of their plans to attend the meetings, and they felt that they had his tacit approval—"We were given a wink and a nod."

Comment

After the Vatican officially permitted (but did not mandate) the use of female altar servers in 1994, only two dioceses in the United States continued to prohibit their use. The bishop of one diocese and a majority of the diocesan priests apparently favored retaining the ban based on their conviction that utilizing only male servers encouraged vocations to the priesthood. Since the rule permitting female servers allowed for local option, the continued prohibition could correctly be described as "a legitimate church practice."

The principle of subsidiary function has been long cherished in Catholic social teaching. It affirms that a community of a higher order should not interfere in the internal life of a community of a lower order, depriving the later of its functions. In this instance, subsidiarity might indicate that each parish be permitted to make its own determinations about who can serve at its altar or meet in its facilities. The case also illustrates the danger of conflict when "mixed messages" are sent.

D. THE RIGHT TO BEAR WITNESS TO AND SPREAD THE GOSPEL MESSAGE

Explanation

It might seem strange to speak of evangelization as a right. After all, Jesus himself, just before his ascension into heaven, commanded his followers to "Go into all the world and proclaim the good news to the whole creation" (Mark 16:15). Since that time, Christians have considered evangelization to be an obligation and a privilege. But a right? Yet the church clearly states that all the Christian faithful have the duty and *right* to work so that the divine message of salvation may increasingly reach all people in every age and in every land (c. 211).

Bearing witness to Christ and his gospel is indeed a primary obligation of the church and of every one of its members (*LG* 17).

But the church insists that it is also a right, and it does so to underline the fact that all of the faithful can and must take the initiative to spread the Christian message. They do not need to wait for the call of the church's hierarchy to do so.

In other words, the right and duty to evangelize is inherent in our baptism and confirmation (c. 879), in our very belonging to the people of God. By the fact of our full communion in the church we have the right and duty to witness to Christ, by ourselves or in our communities. We are all called to exercise Christ's mission in the world (c. 204.1). We do not require a special invitation to engage in our own Christian witness. We are empowered and urged to it by Christ through his Holy Spirit, the Spirit of truth (John 16). Evangelization, that is, proclaiming the message of Christ by word and the witness of our lives, is our native right as baptized Christians (*LG* 35).

The hierarchy of the church, that is, bishops, priests, and deacons, has a key role in coordinating, stimulating, assisting, and even monitoring the manifold works of Christian witness, but every member of the church is responsible too, each one in her or his own place and time. It might be an example given by a parent to a child, or an argument for fairness at work, or teaching in a religious education program, or a contribution to help send a missionary to a non-Christian land—each one of us has a right and a duty to witness to our faith.

Laypersons are singled out for special attention in this regard. The canon merits quoting:

> Since, like all the Christian faithful, lay persons are designated by God for the apostolate through baptism and confirmation, they are bound by the general obligation and possess the right as individuals, or joined in associations, to work so that the divine message of salvation is made known and accepted by all persons everywhere in the

world. This obligation is even more compelling in those circumstances in which only through them [i.e., laypersons] can people hear the gospel and know Christ. (c. 225)

ILLUSTRATION

The Catholic Action movement in the middle of the twentieth century provides an illustrative contrast to this right of evangelization. Catholic Action was initiated and promoted by Pope Pius XI, who was pope from 1922 until 1939. He tried very hard to enlist lay Catholics in a struggle to advance the kingdom of God on this earth. He worked at stimulating and animating the laity in this conscious promotion of the cause of Christ in the secular world. The Catholic Action movement enjoyed considerable success. It was one of the first great modern apostolic movements.

But Catholic Action was always described as "the participation of the laity in the apostolate of the hierarchy." It was the bishops and priests who had the obligation to push the Christian witness, and they elected to enroll the laity in their project in order to advance it. The laity became willing instruments in the hands of the hierarchy, thus extending the influence of the hierarchy.

That vision of the lay role was transcended at the Second Vatican Council. Laypersons were seen to be empowered by the sacraments of initiation, baptism, confirmation, and Eucharist, not deputized by church authorities (LG 33). Hence the declaration of the right of the laity to make known the Christian message.

Now we experience the phenomenon of organizations or movements that are initiated and sustained largely by laypersons, like Voice of the Faithful, Catholics United for the Faith, and the National Leadership Roundtable on Church

Management. Perhaps even more praiseworthy are the thousands of local initiatives by parishes reaching out a helping hand to needy partner communities in poorer countries—not just sending money, but personally building a school in Uganda, supplying a clinic in Haiti, supporting a food program in Guatemala. These grassroots initiatives yield huge benefits for both the sending and receiving communities of faith. They constitute a genuine witness to the gospel of Christ.

Further Reading

The apostolic exhortation of Pope Paul VI, *Evangelization in the Modern World* (*Evangelii Nuntiandi*, December 8, 1975), provides an excellent background for this right and suggests many ways to exercise it.

E. THE RIGHT TO AUTONOMY IN TEMPORAL AFFAIRS

Explanation

The church strongly affirms the autonomy of its members in the temporal order, that is, in matters of family, work, or profession, in the economic, social, cultural, and political arenas. Lay members of the faithful are especially acknowledged to have this right to freedom "in the affairs of the earthly city" (c. 227).

The Second Vatican Council taught repeatedly that the secular order was the rightful domain of the laity:

- It is the special vocation of the laity to seek the kingdom of God by engaging in temporal affairs and ordering them in accordance with the will of God (*LG* 31).

- The laity have the principal role, through their secular activity, in the task of permeating the world with the spirit of Christ, so that it can attain its purpose in justice, love, and peace (*LG* 36).

- Laypersons, living in the midst of the world and engaged in secular affairs, are to permeate the temporal order with the spirit of the gospel, and thus to perfect it; they are a leaven in the world (*AA* 2).

- In the pilgrimage of this life the laity will devote themselves to informing the temporal order of things with the Christian spirit and perfecting it (*AA* 4).

- Laypeople should take the restoration of the secular order as their proper function and work at it directly, led by the light of the gospel (*AA* 7).

- The laity are to imbue the world with a Christian spirit, and are to be witnesses to Christ in all they do within human society (*GS* 43).

Priests and those in religious life are also involved in and share responsibility for the temporal order, but they are admonished to refrain from certain secular involvements, such as civil offices, businesses and trades, political parties, and labor unions (cc. 285–287, 672). All of the ordained clergy are to acknowledge and promote the laity in the exercise of their mission in the church and in the world (c. 275.2).

The right to autonomy and freedom in the secular order is to be exercised in communion, that is, not in sublime independence and disregard for the church and its teachings but with a sense of being a part of the body of Christ. Canon 227 says that when using this freedom laypersons are to take care that their actions are imbued with the spirit of the gospel and are to pay attention to the teachings of church authorities.

On the other hand, the church respects diversity of views. It goes without saying that Catholics differ on many matters of policy and practice, even when they are earnestly seeking to follow the gospel. Such legitimate differences of opinion are not uncommon. Sincere dialogue, mutual charity, and concern for the common good should prevail.

EXAMPLE

The debate in Congress over the use of embryonic stem cells for medical research is a case in point. There are many Catholic lawmakers on both sides of the issue. The church opposes the destruction of innocent human life and the process of in vitro fertilization, but there are genuine differences of opinion when it comes to the legitimacy and wisdom of using federal funds for experiments on human embryos donated by couples who no longer need them for their fertility treatments.

The embryos in question were obtained in efforts to conceive, and those not used will be destroyed in any event. The embryos are human, but were never implanted. Is it permissible or prudent to use them in a search for cures for several serious diseases? Privately funded research and even some state funded research of this sort is already under way.

While the moral principle of the value of human life must be held secure, is the use of embryonic stem cells for medical research the kind of public policy issue, complex and cutting edge, and in a very pluralistic society, on which even thoughtful and prayerful Catholics can legitimately disagree?

Further Reading

Pope John Paul II issued an apostolic exhortation, *The Vocation and the Mission of the Lay Faithful in the Church and in the World* (December 30, 1988), which speaks to the right of freedom of action in the secular order.

F. THE RIGHT TO USE ONE'S GIFTS FROM THE HOLY SPIRIT (CHARISMS)

Explanation

Charisms are gifts or special graces given to the faithful by the Holy Spirit for the building up of the church or for use "in the world." Some are associated with offices in the church, like the charism of infallibility with the office of the papacy, but others are freely given by the Spirit to individuals or groups. Some are extraordinary and unusual, as in St. Paul's references to the gifts of healing, prophecy, mighty deeds, and speaking in tongues (1 Cor 12), while others are simpler, ordinary, or rather routine, as in the patience of a mother, the clarity of a teacher, or the organizational ability of an administrator.

The Second Vatican Council stated quite clearly that the Holy Spirit gives special gifts to the faithful, and that they are to use them for service. "Through receiving these gifts of grace, however unspectacular, every one of the faithful has the right and duty to exercise them in the church and in the world, for the good of humanity and the building up of the church" (*AA* 3). They do this in the freedom of the Spirit who blows where the Spirit wills (John 3:8) and, at the same time, in communion with their brothers and sisters in Christ.

Hence the right to exercise charisms is undisputed, even though, surprisingly, this right did not find explicit expression in the 1983 Code of Canon Law. But the use of charisms must always respect the situation and needs of the larger community. Charisms are given by the Spirit for the benefit of the church, and must not become sources of conflict or division within it. It is for this reason that the council documents insist that judgment about the authenticity and ordered use of charisms belongs to those who preside over the church. They are to take care not to extinguish the Spirit, but to test everything and hold on to what is good (*LG* 7, 12; *AA* 3).

ILLUSTRATIONS

The church throughout its long history has always been charismatic, but that charismatic element is not always to be sought solely in what is very rare and extraordinary. There is much more that is charismatic than one at first might think. We see it in hidden fidelity, unselfish kindness, sincerity of disposition, purity of heart, courage that does duty without fuss; the uncompromising profession of truth, the inexpressible love of a soul for God, the unshakable trust of a sinner that God's heart is greater than ours and that God is rich in mercy; the goodness of a patient nursing sister, serving, praying, asking nothing else of life; good mothers whose virtue is a gift from the Spirit, a reflection of God's unselfish love.

Ultimately the church exists so that witness may be borne to the eternal significance of these things, so that there may always be people who really and seriously believe that these gifts are more important than anything else.

(An edited summary of Karl Rahner's "The Charistmatic Element in the Church," *The Dynamic Element in the Church* [New York: Herder & Herder, 1964], 62–66.)

Comments

The phenomenon of gifts that differ and their exercise for the benefit of the church (Rom 12:6–8) is nowhere more pronounced today than in the proliferation of the church's ministries. Charisms are distinct from our human talents (bright, artistic), from our Christian virtues (loving, forgiving), from our vocation or state in life (married, religious), and from our office in the church (pastor, religion teacher), but charisms can be related to all of these. Charisms are gifts from the Holy Spirit for the benefit of the church or the world; they are ways in which the Spirit endows or gives ability to Christian individuals or groups for specific actions, to fulfill specific services. Charisms are added gifts. In addition to talents, virtues, and callings, charisms are the "something more" that persons bring to ministry. Dorothy Day and Peter Maurin come to mind as examples of contemporary American charismatics.

Another manifestation of the Spirit's charisms in the church, both historically and at present, is seen in the various movements that have profoundly influenced the church and the world. Historical examples include early monasticism, medieval mendicant and evangelical initiatives, sixteenth-century missionaries, and modern apostolic congregations. Contemporary examples are some of the lay movements like Catholic Action, the St. Vincent de Paul Society, the Community of St. Egidio, and Voice of the Faithful.

4. RIGHTS RELATED TO ONE'S STATE IN LIFE

A. THE RIGHT TO FREELY CHOOSE A STATE IN LIFE

Explanation

All the Christian faithful have the right to be free from any kind of coercion in choosing a state of life (c. 219). The right is stated as an immunity; it is intended to protect the freedom of persons to choose their own vocation or personal destiny. This right is derived from the dignity of the human person, and, in the church's teaching, it is listed along with other universal and inviolable rights, such as the rights to food, clothing, shelter, and education and the right to found a family (GS 26).

Church teaching goes on to urge the elimination of all kinds of discrimination affecting the fundamental rights of persons, specifically when women are denied the choice of a husband or state of life or opportunities for education equal to those available to men (GS 29). Parents and educators are charged with assisting children and young people to develop in such a way as to be able to exercise full responsibility in following their own calling, not pushing them directly or indirectly into marriage or a choice of partner (GS 52).

The church's regulations specify protections of vocational freedom of choice:

- Marriage is a basic right of all persons (c. 1058), and a man and a woman enter into the marriage covenant by means of their mutual free consent (cc. 1057, 1103). Indeed, in order to safeguard the freedom to marry, the church provides for a marriage to be entered into before lay witnesses alone if a priest or deacon is not available (c. 1116).

- Laypersons enjoy the right to remain single, simply because of their own choice or for the sake of the kingdom of God, that is, for personal, spiritual, or apostolic reasons (cc. 225, 227).

- A person must possess due freedom in order to be ordained to the diaconate, priesthood, or episcopate (c. 1026); candidates for the diaconate or priesthood must attest in their own handwriting that they will receive the order freely and of their own accord (c. 1036).

- Similarly, no one may be induced to enter a religious community by means of force, fear, or fraud (c. 643.1, #4).

In our liberated culture, abuses of this freedom to choose one's own state of life are relatively rare, at least in contrast to cultures in which arranged marriages are the norm; but sometimes persons feel pressured into marriage because of pregnancy, poverty, or the desire to escape from an abusive home. Historically, it was not uncommon for children whom their parents judged to be unmarriageable to be forced into a convent or monastery.

The right to choose freely one's state in life and to found a family is a fundamental human right (GS 26), as well as a right of all Christians that is explicitly recognized by the church (c. 219).

It can sometimes come into conflict with the church's other regulations; for example, when a person who was previously married desires to marry again and is certain that the prior marriage was not valid, the church forbids the remarriage until the nullity of the prior marriage has been established according to church law (c. 1085.2). However, if the church's legal process is not available to the person or is extremely burdensome, the basic right to marry prevails.

CASE

Patricia met Steve at a party in Denver in 1990. She had been in the city for just a few months and had a low-paying job that barely allowed her to subsist. She had come to Denver from a small town in Kansas mainly to get away from home, where her abusive stepmother had made her life miserable. Patricia was twenty-four and had been a Catholic all her life.

Steve was a native of Denver, but he lived overseas. He was back in the city only for a visit. He was an engineer with a large construction company, and he loved his work. Steve was a baptized Presbyterian, but did not really practice his religion. He was twenty-seven.

Patricia and Steve went on a couple of dates, but within a few days Steve flew off to his job in India. They corresponded frequently and grew more and more interested in one another. After several months Steve persuaded Patricia to meet him in Australia for a ten-day holiday. They got along well and had a good time together. After the first few days they made love, and they did so several more times during the rest of the visit.

For Patricia, their sexual relations meant a commitment. She had never made love with anyone else and after her experience with Steve she was determined to marry him. A few months later, after may letters and telephone calls, Steve agreed to marry.

It was several more months before Steve could get home for the wedding. They were married at St. Mary's Catholic Church in Denver on June 29, 1992. They got along fine for a while, but Steve was away working at various sites overseas more than half of the time. They had a baby girl late in 1993. Although Steve loved the baby, most of her care fell to Patricia because of Steve's absences. He was completely dedicated to his work; everything else—including his family—was secondary.

Patricia began to realize that neither one of them had gotten to know the other. They never had the chance to really grow together, to take the measure of the other and make adjustments for the other's personality. Steve didn't seem to want to make the effort, and he wouldn't even consider changing his work pattern. Patricia began to lose interest in their marriage. They separated in 2001, and were divorced the next year.

In 2004 Patricia met someone else, a Catholic widower five years older than she, who fell in love with her and her daughter and wanted to marry Patricia. Patricia was—and remains—convinced that her marriage to Steve was never valid. Realizing that her circumstances had pressured her into marrying Steve and that he was always actually married to his job, Patricia tried to bring a petition for the annulment of her marriage to the Denver Tribunal (marriage court), but Steve and her own parents refuse to have anything to do with it.

Now it looks as though she may not be able to get a declaration of nullity from the church in order to marry her Catholic friend, despite her best efforts.

Comment

Will Patricia's fundamental right to marry prevail? She may be able to persuade the tribunal to grant her an annulment based on her own testimony and that of a couple of character witnesses. Or she may be able to find a priest who will concur with her judgment that her marriage to Steve was not valid, and who will witness her marriage even though she does not obtain an annulment from a tribunal.

B. THE RIGHT TO RESPONSIBLE PARENTHOOD

Explanation

Marriage and married love by their nature are directed toward the begetting and bringing up of children. Hence, the procreation and education of children are among the principal purposes of marriage, along with the good of the couple and their mutuality in sharing all of life together in a loving partnership.

The spouses have the right as well as the responsibility to conceive, bear, and rear children according to their own prayerful judgment of their situation and economic means. The church's teaching on responsible parenthood clearly implies the right of the spouses to plan for their family, including the number and spacing of their children. The Vatican Council as well as subsequent papal teachings explicitly acknowledge this right and freedom of married couples regarding the transmission of life (*GS* 50–52, *HV* 10, *FC* 30, 34, 46).

The more controversial issues regarding the *means* used by couples in exercising this right and responsibility must not be allowed to obscure or overshadow the basic right itself. Natural family planning and the various other methods of regulating conception are critical interpersonal and moral issues, but they are secondary to the fundamental right of the married couple to responsible parenthood.

CASE

The drums of war were beating. Everyone in the world knew that the administration was determined to go to war with Iraq in order to depose its dictator. For Mike and Sally, an Army lieutenant and his wife, this posed a very personal dilemma. Mike's unit was surely going to be one of the first to go into Iraq. It would be very dangerous and, although everyone was confident about the outcome, no one knew how long it would take or how many men and women would be killed or wounded.

Sally and Mike were in their early thirties and had two young children, Amy, four, and Tim, two. They had always planned to have at least three or four children. They thought they could afford that many and they wanted to have them while they were still young, healthy, and energetic. They thought it better for the children's development if they were relatively close in age. So they were ready to have their third child now, but then came this talk of war.

They agonized over their decision. What if Mike were away for a prolonged tour of duty? What if, God forbid, he were killed or seriously wounded? Wouldn't the prudent thing be to postpone the third child until the war was over and Mike was safely home?

Comment

Christian marriage is both a *natural* community of intimate sharing of life and love instituted by the Creator and a *sacramental* union reflecting Christ's loving union with his church, the people for whom he gave his life. Christian partners are strengthened and consecrated for the duties of their married life by this sacrament, by virtue of which they fulfill their marital and parental tasks with the aid of the Holy Spirit (*GS* 48). This is the profoundly religious context within which spouses should view the rights and responsibilities of procreation and formation of their children. The spouses are not alone; they have the support of God's grace and of their Christian community. Sally and Mike should draw upon both sources of support as they prayerfully discern the answer to their dilemma.

C. THE RIGHT TO EDUCATE CHILDREN

Explanation

To put this right in perspective, we must recall that all persons have an inalienable right to education; it is one of the basic human rights that flow from the dignity of the human person (*GE* 1). Then we need to recognize that the Christian faithful have the right to a Christian education, since they are called to lead lives in keeping with the teachings of the gospel (c. 217). When it comes to the education of children and young people, the question arises: Who provides their general education and who provides their Christian education? Who has those rights and corresponding obligations?

The church's answer to these questions is quite clear: parents have the primary responsibility for the education of their children, since they conferred life on them. Parents have a very serious obligation and possess the right to educate their children (c. 226.2); they are their primary and principal educators (*GE* 3). Therefore it is the parents who must also see to the

Christian education of their children as well, a formation that is in keeping with the teachings of the church.

The regulations of the church spell out in detail these parental rights and duties:

- Parents are obliged to form their children by word and example in faith and in the practice of Christian life (c. 774.2).

- Parents have not only the obligation and right to educate their offspring, but also the right and duty to choose the means and institutions most suitable for their Christian education in their local circumstances (c. 793.1).

- Parents should be free to choose schools for their children, preferably those that provide a Catholic education, but if that is not possible, then they should provide for their children's Catholic education outside the schools (cc. 797–798).

- Parents are to see to their children's sacramental formation and initiation, baptism, confirmation, and First Communion (cc. 851.2, 867.1, 890, 914).

Though parents have a primary right and obligation to see to the development and education, both general and Christian, of their children, others—i.e., civil society and the church—share those responsibilities as well. Cities and states provide school systems to support and supplement the parents' role. The church and its pastoral ministers cooperate and assist parents, especially in the Catholic formation of their children (*GE* 3).

The rules of the church make reference to its pastoral responsibilities in several places, such as in the canons on catechetical formation and sacramental preparation of children (cc. 776, 777, 843.2, 914), as well as in the canons that deal with Catholic education more generally (cc. 794, 800).

In sum, the vital and challenging task of education and Christian formation at its best is a work of harmonious collaboration between families, civil societies, and church communities. These should be rights exercised in coordination—not in competition—for the common goal, namely the formation and full development of each human person.

CASE

Sarah was a lifelong and staunch Catholic, but at the same time she was strongly pro-choice. She was convinced that abortion should be retained as a safe and lawful option in the United States, but made as rare as possible by providing preventive measures and alternative choices for women with unplanned pregnancies. Sarah was married to John, also a Catholic and quietly supportive of Sarah's view on abortion. They sent all of their children to Catholic schools.

When Sarah and John's eldest child, Jane, was thirteen and just about to enter eighth grade at their parish school, she joined her mother at a march in the state capital in support of some pro-choice legislation. Jane was pictured in the local newspaper the next day standing beside her mother and carrying a pro-choice banner. Father Schmidt, their pastor, was outraged when he saw the photo. He immediately notified Sarah and John that Jane was no longer welcome in the parish grade school, and he cancelled her registration for the fall semester.

Sarah and John tried to reason with Father Schmidt, but he was adamant. They appealed to the diocesan superintendent of schools and then to the bishop, but neither of them was willing to overrule the pastor's decision, even though they disagreed with his action. They didn't want to send the wrong message on the abortion issue.

Questions

Should the pastor have talked to the family before taking action? Should Jane, an adolescent, have been punished for what was obviously her mother's initiative, even if Jane was a willing participant in the march? Was expulsion from the parish school an appropriate action? Did it infringe on Jane's parents' right to educate her?

D. THE RIGHT TO JUST WAGES AND BENEFITS

Explanation

The right of church employees to decent family wages and benefits is one of the most clearly and strongly stated of all rights of Catholics in the church. In fact, it is stated twice in the 1983 Code of Canon Law. (Indeed, it was already called for in canon 1524 of the 1917 Code of Canon Law.)

First, among the "rights of the lay Christian faithful," the Code states that laypersons employed by the church either permanently or temporarily "have the right to fair remuneration appropriate to their condition so that they are able to provide decently for their own needs and those of their family. They also have a right for their social provision [retirement benefits], social security, and health benefits to be duly provided" (c. 231.2).

Second, in the section on the administration of church property, administrators are charged:

- in the employment of workers to observe the principles of the church's social justice tradition as well as the civil laws on labor and social policy, and

- "to pay a just and decent wage to employees so that they are able to provide fittingly for their own needs and those of their dependents" (c. 1286).

The right to organize unions for collective bargaining is clearly affirmed in the church's teaching documents. The right of workers to freely form associations to represent them is among the basic rights of the human person, and so is the right to take part freely in union activities without fear of reprisal (GS 68). Church employees are not excluded.

Laypersons, quite naturally, are the principal focus of this right to just family remuneration, but ordained ministers too have a canonical claim to a suitable remuneration, health care, and old age assistance (c. 281).

ILLUSTRATION

In view of the church's insistence on the right to a just wage and benefits, the opposition of some groups in the church to organized collective bargaining seems surprising and puzzling. For example, some diocesan school systems and some hospitals sponsored by religious communities have strenuously resisted the efforts of teachers and nurses to form unions. Clearly there are economic consequences to unionization, and some fear that it might cause a partial loss of control over both personnel and policy in the schools and hospitals. Still, the vigor and persistence, not to say bitterness, of the opposition appears anomalous in light of the church's teachings on this area of social justice.

Comment

The church's social justice tradition is embodied in a series of papal documents from Leo XIII's *On the Condition of Workers*

(*Rerum Novarum*, 1891) to John Paul II's *The One Hundredth Year* (*Centesimus Annus*, 1991) as well as in the Vatican Council's *Pastoral Constitution on the Church in the Modern World* (*Gaudium et Spes*, 1965) and the American bishops' *Economic Justice for All: Pastoral Letter on Catholic Social Teaching and the U.S. Economy* (1986). All of them attend to just conditions for workers.

5. RIGHTS TO FORMATION AND EDUCATION

A. THE RIGHT TO FORM AND FOLLOW ONE'S CONSCIENCE

Explanation

The Second Vatican Council forcefully reaffirmed the crucial role of conscience in Christian moral decision-making.

> Deep within their conscience individuals discover a law which they do not make for themselves but which they are bound to obey, whose voice, ever summoning them to love and do what is good and to avoid what is evil, rings in their hearts when necessary with the command: Do this, keep away from that. For inscribed in their hearts by God, human beings have a law whose observance is their dignity and in accordance with which they are to be judged. Conscience is the most intimate center and sanctuary of a person, in which he or she is alone with God whose voice echoes within them. (GS 16)

> People grasp and acknowledge the precepts of the divine law by means of their own consciences, which they

are bound to follow faithfully in all their activity so as to come to God, their end. (*DH* 3)

Here the council sounded the teaching of the Apostle Paul on the interior law. He said that the Gentiles, who observed the prescriptions of the Mosaic law that was not given to them (but rather to the Jews), "show that what the law requires is written in their hearts." Thus their consciences will bear witness for them when God judges their hidden works through Christ Jesus (Rom 2:14–16). People must therefore not be forced to act against their conscience, nor must they be prevented from acting according to it, especially in religious matters (*DH* 3).

Conscience is not so much an isolated faculty or power within the human person as it is the person herself or himself as morally conscious and morally responsible. It is the person striving to respond to multiple relationships, with others and with God. Conscience describes the human subject as moral agent, searching and reaching toward values, toward authenticity and self-transcendence, in the context of these relationships.

Because it is always the ultimate norm of moral action, conscience must be formed, it must be followed, and it must be free.

Conscience must be formed. Each person has the obligation continually and properly to form her or his conscience by training, reflection, dialogue, and prayer. Formation of conscience is part of the ongoing task of Christian conversion. It takes place within the individual communities that constitute the church. Personal limitations and sinful inclinations are more readily overcome in the context of a community.

Conscience must be followed. One must decide and act in accord with one's own conscience. In this sense conscience is the final norm of morality. One must be true to oneself in order to be authentically Christian. Each person, as an acting subject, must accept the freedom and responsibility that God has given her or him.

Conscience must be free. Constrained conscience is not capable of truly moral activity. If there is no choice to be made, no range of human freedom, then there is no conscientious action, no opportunity for virtue or vice. A coerced compliance or an externally compelled conscience is no conscience at all.

A church community, such as a parish, should strive to assist its members in their moral formation and decision-making. Church communities should be healthy contexts in which mature Christian consciences are supported and can function freely.

In addition, decisions that local churches make should emerge from a collective or "community conscience." Communities, like individuals, are obliged to act conscientiously. They possess a shared moral sense, an estimation of moral values in the context of the pragmatic decision at hand. When a parish decides to close its school or build a parish center or send aid to a parish in Guatemala, it should be a decision of conscience.

CASE

Agnes, a thirty-year member of the Sisters of Mercy, was appointed by the governor to be director of the Department of Social Services of the State of Michigan early in 1983. She accepted the position with the approval of the archbishop of Detroit, whose permission was required by canon law. Late in February the archbishop withdrew his approval and called for Agnes to resign after Agnes failed to state to his satisfaction her opposition to state funding for abortions. The social services agency, in addition to its many other programs for the poor, also oversaw Medicaid funds, which included funding for abortions. Agnes stated her personal opposition to abortion, but the archbishop wanted her to oppose the public funding for abortions. This she was unwilling to do. He considered her refusal to be a source of confusion and scandal to Catholics.

The archbishop reported the matter to the Congregation for Religious in Rome, and in March the Congregation ordered Agnes's religious superior to require Agnes to submit her resignation as director. By this time the conflict had become major national news.

In April Agnes asked for and received a temporary leave of absence from the Sisters of Mercy, and the leadership of the community asked the Congregation for Religious to reconsider its decision. The Congregation promptly delegated an auxiliary bishop of Brooklyn to contact Agnes directly and order her, under her vow of obedience, to resign her position.

The bishop met with Agnes at the provincial house in Farmington Hills, Michigan, on May 9, 1983, and insisted that she resign her position immediately or he would begin proceedings for her dismissal from the community of the Sisters of Mercy. After discussion, reflection, and prayer, Agnes requested a dispensation from her vows and departure from the community. The bishop granted her request on the spot. She was no longer a Sister of Mercy (although she remained an associate member of the order). The community leaders appealed to the Congregation for Religious to reconsider the whole matter but it declined to do so.

Agnes served out the rest of her term as director of social services.

Comment

This case illustrates a conflict between the personal conscience of a Catholic woman religious and the concerns of church authority for moral teaching and the appearance of cooperation in immoral activity. Agnes felt justified in conscience taking a position that tolerated the public funding for abortion in order to avoid even greater harm if the funding was not available to the poor. She saw it as a legitimate disagreement over a matter of public policy. The archbishop and the Congregation viewed it as a compromise of serious church teaching on the evil of abortion. They also felt that the very fact of a Catholic religious woman heading an agency that funded abortions gave scandal to the Catholic faithful. The authorities were able to enforce their views and in doing so they removed her from her religious community. Agnes stood by her conscience, but at great personal cost.

B. THE RIGHT TO CHRISTIAN FORMATION AND EDUCATION

Explanation

Since the faithful are called to lead lives in keeping with the teachings of the gospel, they have the right to a Christian education (c. 217). This right is rooted in the fact that Christians have been made a new creation, born of water and the Holy Spirit, and truly are children of God (GE 2). Christian education has a twofold aim, namely to help people achieve maturity as human persons and to assist them in gaining knowledge of the mysteries of salvation so that they can live in accord with them.

All persons have an inalienable right to education, and one that is suited to their own abilities, their culture, and their tradition (*GE* 1). Added to this basic human right is the right to a religious education, and specifically to a Christian education. Parents have the primary responsibility for the education of their children; the Christian family is the first and most effective school. Then it is the responsibility of the local Catholic community to provide further formation in Christ, to offer an appropriate catechesis for both children and adults so that their faith becomes living, explicit, and operative.

The church's canons are unusually detailed in spelling out these formative rights and obligations (cc. 226.2, 229, 528.1, 773–780, 793–795, 843.2). The formation of its members is a vital part of the church's teaching function and of the life of the local Christian community. Formation is a challenging task in which we all share. Christian education is accomplished in schools and programs of religious instruction, but also in the liturgy, in preaching, in sacramental preparation programs (especially the Rite of Christian Initiation of Adults, First Communion, and confirmation), and in many parish outreach and evangelization programs. The various forms of print and electronic media also play their roles.

CASE

Michael and Mary Harmon are dedicated to home-schooling their four children. Mary had some experience as a teacher, and the family lives in a rural section of Kansas, a long way from good schools, Catholic or public. They are a devout Catholic family.

When their eldest child, Chris, was thirteen, the couple told their pastor that they wanted to have him confirmed with the other children of the parish when the bishop came in April. The pastor referred the Harmons to the parish director of religious education. The DRE insisted that the couple send Chris to the parish program that prepared the children for confirmation. Michael and Mary demurred, for logistical reasons of time and distance, and for educational reasons; they were convinced that they were preparing Chris for the sacrament very well. They said that the text they were using with Chris, although different from the text used in the parish program, was one that was approved by the American bishops.

The DRE was adamant, fearing that the Harmons were forming their children in an isolated context that would foster a privatized view of religion, and he was apprehensive that an exception for Chris would lead to many more defections from the parish program. The pastor was forced to adjudicate the dispute between the Harmons and the DRE. He acknowledged the priority of parental rights in the formation of their children, but he also pointed out that the church too has a responsibility to form its members within its own community. He managed to work out a compromise that permitted Chris to receive confirmation with the others.

Comment

This case illustrates the real conflicts that can occur in the exercise of rights, those of responsible parents as over against those of a responsible pastor and parish staff. Far more than hurt feelings are at stake in a situation like this; whole families can be alienated from the church, whole formation programs can be destroyed. Careful and objective procedures can help create a successful solution. For example, the parish staff might engage the Harmons in extended conversations to discern what their religious views and practices are. The staff might compare the two texts to see if there are serious discrepancies, and they might consult the diocesan office to learn of precedents or compromises. The goal is not to win a fight, but to see that Chris is well prepared for fruitful reception of the sacrament.

C. THE RIGHT TO THEOLOGICAL INQUIRY AND EXPRESSION

Explanation

The freedom of theological investigation and expression is a right explicitly recognized by the church (c. 218). This right is vital not only to the effective work of the theological community but also to the successful function of the church's teaching authority, for it is the theologians who contribute most to the development of the church's doctrine and to its effective communication to the people of today (*GS* 62).

The right to pursue theological investigation and to publish the results of those efforts is a specific instance of the right of religious liberty, a fundamental human right acknowledged by the church. This basic right includes the duty to seek religious truth, to embrace it freely, and to honor it by observance (*DH* 1–2). The right to communicate the findings of theological inquiry is also a specific application of the basic freedom of expression, another fundamental human right recognized by the church (c. 212.2–3). In addition, it is an extension of the right to education (c. 217), for higher education cannot succeed without proper freedom of scientific inquiry (*GE* 10).

Within the community of faith this theological freedom is central to the church's teaching function in which all of the faithful rightfully participate (c. 204.1).

Those engaged in the sacred disciplines enjoy this freedom and right (c. 218). "Sacred disciplines" describes a cluster of theologically related fields of study including biblical studies, moral theology, church history, canon law, and pastoral studies as well as dogmatic or systematic theology.

The persons engaged in these disciplines, whether lay, religious, or ordained, whether teaching in colleges, universities, or seminaries, or otherwise employed, are to exercise this right:

- appropriately, that is, with due regard for the profession of faith, the most basic tenets of the Catholic Church;

- prudently, humbly, and courageously, in keeping with professional standards;

- within their own area of training and expertise; and

- observing the respect due to the church's teaching authority (see c. 218).

The protection for and exercise of this right to theological inquiry and expression are especially important in the Catholic Church, which values the integrity and continuity of its doctrinal tradition so highly. Hence the exercise of this precious freedom must always be viewed with regard to the hierarchy of truths, the fact that truths vary in their connection to the foundations of the Christian faith, some being much more central than others (*UR* 11). There must be an awareness that the profession of a common faith is one of the bonds of our communion (c. 205). Within these parameters, respectful disagreement with official teaching is not only possible, but sometimes necessary, if indeed theologians are to illuminate the faith of the church, preserve the legitimate diversity within the church, and contribute to the development of its teaching (CCEO, cc. 604, 606).

Finally, it should be noted that this right of theological freedom is one of the very few rights that diocesan bishops are specifically charged to defend (c. 386.2).

CASE

The Charles E. Curran case, which was played out at The Catholic University of America from 1979 to 1986, was a classic confrontation over the limits of theological freedom. The protagonists were the Congregation for the Doctrine of the Faith in Rome and Curran, a highly regarded and prolific tenured professor of moral theology at the university. The central issue in the conflict was the competence of church's official teaching authority as over against the ability of a theologian to disagree with that authority on specific matters of moral teaching. Several other issues of moral methodology and specific moral questions were included in this protracted "dialogue," but the basic problem was the role of the teaching authority versus a theologian's right to dissent from teachings that are acknowledged to be non-infallible, that is, reformable.

After hundreds of pages of written correspondence and one informal meeting in Rome, the issue of the extent or limits of permissible dissent was not really clarified. On July 25, 1986, the Congregation took the position toward Curran "that one who dissents from the Magisterium as you do is not suitable nor eligible to teach Catholic Theology."

Curran was forced to leave Catholic University in 1987, and for many years has taught as a tenured university professor at Southern Methodist University. He continues to write and speak extensively on Catholic theology.

Comment

The Congregation for the Doctrine of the Faith issued an instruction on May 24, 1990, entitled "On the Ecclesial Vocation
of Theologian." The document stated that the freedom proper
to theological research is exercised within the church's faith.
The church's teaching authority makes pronouncements of various kinds: infallible, definitive, and non-definitive declarations,
or simply interventions on questions under discussion. These
levels of teaching obviously call for very different levels of response from the theologian: from the assent of faith to a judgment that a given intervention is deficient and mistaken.

The document allowed for the possibility that a theologian
might have legitimate difficulties and disagreements with the
declarations of church teaching authority, and it suggested appropriate ways of expressing such disagreement. But the instruction went on to characterize *dissent* as an attitude of general opposition to church teaching that takes diverse forms, but
whose modes, motivations, and methodologies are all mis-
guided. (This characterization of dissent is not shared by most
of the Catholic theological community.)

The instruction urged theologians to seek solutions to their
difficulties in trustful dialogue with church authorities in the
spirit of truth and charity that is proper to the communion of
the church.

6. RIGHTS TO DUE PROCESS

A. THE RIGHT TO VINDICATE AND DEFEND RIGHTS IN THE CHURCH

Explanation

The church asserts that all the faithful can claim or protect their rights in the church before a competent legal, that is, canonical, forum, in either a judicial or an administrative procedure (c. 221.1). The court or administrator must have competence to judge the parties or the matter at issue (cc. 1408–1418). The first purpose of a judicial trial is the pursuit or vindication of rights, those of individuals or those of legal entities (i.e., juridic persons, such as parishes or dioceses; c. 1400.1).

Access to a procedure to vindicate or defend one's rights is a basic and key element of any legal system. It is one of the ways that the church shows respect for the human person, now fully incorporated into the communion of faith. Human rights that are merely stated but not protected by some sort of due process of law remain rights in theory, with little practical value.

This assertion of the right to claim one's rights should not be seen as an encouragement to litigate. Quite the contrary, the church, following the gospels, explicitly discourages litigious disputes. Jesus said, "Come to terms quickly with your accuser while you are on the way to court with him" (Matt 5:25). The faithful, and bishops in particular, are urged to avoid litigation as much as possible and to resolve disputes peacefully and expeditiously (c. 1446.1). The church's regulations strongly recommend processes of conciliation, mediation, or arbitration in order to avoid litigation or conflict (cc. 1446.2–3, 1733).

Most of the church's governing activity is administrative, that is, it involves the exercise of executive authority, rather than judicial or legislative power. When someone is aggrieved by the administrative action of a person in authority, then the pursuit of justice or the vindication of one's right is called administrative *recourse* (cc. 1732–1739).

But before one takes recourse to the superior of the person who took the offensive administrative action, one should first ask that person in writing to reconsider the action (c. 1734.1). "If another member of the church sins against you, go and point out the fault when the two of you are alone" (Matt 18:15).

Some matters under dispute may be taken directly to a church court by means of a written petition to a judge. The first instance of such ecclesiastical courts or tribunals operates at the level of the diocese, but there are also higher courts to which judicial *appeals* can be made. However, as a matter of fact, most diocesan tribunals concern themselves only with the adjudication of matrimonial petitions, that is, requests for the annulment of marriages. They are not open, most often, to claims or defenses of other rights of the faithful.

CASE

Father Gregory was fifty-nine years old and had been pastor of Sacred Heart parish for ten years. It was his fourth pastorate. He was a pretty good pastor, but he tended to be overbearing in public, and he had a temper. He had hired several pastoral staff members over the years, and some were not strong persons. He treated them well in most respects, but sometimes he would berate them in public. Later he would say that he just liked to blow off steam. He was well known around the diocese for these tirades.

Father Gregory was granted a sabbatical leave to go away for a semester of studies in 2001. While he was away, the parish staff members bonded more closely and shared their dissatisfaction with their pastor. Five of them wrote to the bishop complaining about the pastor's treatment of them and saying that they couldn't deal with him any longer. They asked the bishop to replace Father Gregory. The bishop was preoccupied with other matters, and he wrote back saying that he would deal with the matter when the pastor returned from his sabbatical.

The five staff members were both irritated at what they perceived to be the bishop's brush-off and alarmed at the prospect of the pastor's return. They sought out an aggressive lawyer who characterized Father Gregory's actions as "serious verbal abuse in the workplace." The lawyer demanded that the bishop remove the pastor. Otherwise, the lawyer's clients would sue the pastor and the diocese in civil court, Father Gregory for intentional infliction of mental distress and the diocese for negligent supervision. They weren't asking for money damages or any other punishment, only that Father Gregory be removed from the parish.

At this point the complaint was referred to the diocesan office of due process, headed by Janet Devon. Janet asked the bishop to give Father Gregory a one-month extension of his sabbatical leave, which he did. Janet met with

the staff members and their attorney, listened to their grievances, and apologized to them in the name of the diocese
for the pastor's behavior. She persuaded them to enter the
diocese's process for dispute resolution. Janet advised them
that the civil court would probably insist that they exhaust
that avenue of recourse before accepting their complaint,
because the process had been in place for years, was used
regularly, and was successful in 80 percent of its cases.

Janet insisted that Father Gregory be a full participant
in the proceedings and provided him with able canonical
council at diocesan expense. She then obtained the services of a retired judge who was an experienced mediator.
All of the parties came to the table and hashed out their differences. Because the preparations had been thorough, the
mediation went forward to a resolution in a single day. Father Gregory, with the help of his canonical counselor, was
able to see the consequences of his actions and agreed to
resign. He began anger counseling and was made administrator of another parish. The staff members were satisfied
and went ahead to work with a new pastor.

Comment

The procedure used in the case and the outcome it achieved is
called "restorative justice." Restorative justice strives to go beyond finding winners and losers and fixing blame; it focuses on
relationships between people and brings healing to the community. Not all conflicts work out as well as this case did, but
restorative justice strives for such results by bringing the parties
together in a facilitated dialogue.

B. THE RIGHT TO BE JUDGED
ACCORDING TO CANON LAW AND WITH EQUITY

Explanation

If a member of the faithful, whether layperson, religious, or ordained, is summoned before church authority for judgment, she or he has the right to be judged according to the law, with all of the safeguards that the law provides (c. 221.2). This basic rule of justice refers to canon law, the law of the church. In other words, no one is to be subjected to arbitrary or capricious judgment, but must be judged according to the church's canonical rules.

Moreover, not only must the rule of law prevail when a person is brought to judgment, but the law is to be applied with equity. In canon law, equity has a long history and enjoys high esteem. Canonical equity means not merely that the law must be applied justly and fairly; it must also be applied with mercy. The rigor of the law is to be tempered with Christian charity. Even in giving judgment, the church's action must manifest and serve the life of the Spirit. It must be seen as carrying on the saving activity of Christ.

The previous section (immediately above) on "The Right to Vindicate and Defend Rights" assumes that a member of the church is taking the initiative, is bringing a legal action, is petitioning authority in pursuit of his or her rights. Here, on the other hand, the presumption is that the person is responding to a claim, is the one being summoned, is being brought before the authority.

The judgment process in question can be judicial or administrative, that is, the person may be summoned before a judge in a church court or before an administrator outside of court. There are safeguards in both procedures, like the right of self-defense and the right to representation, but they are greater and more detailed in the judicial process.

This right to be judged in accord with canon law is a general norm that has specific application to the church's penal law, where canonical penalties are imposed for canonical crimes.

If a member of the church, whether priest, religious, or layperson, should have the misfortune to commit a canonical crime or to be accused of committing one, and if a church authority is going to take punitive action, the procedure and punishment must be in keeping with the canonical rules (c. 221.3). This canonical action is separate and apart from any legal action that may or may not be taken by civil authorities.

Most canonical crimes are those specifically recognized in the Code of Canon Law (cc. 1364–1398), such as heresy, profaning the Eucharist, perjury, stirring up hatred against the church, simulating the administration of a sacrament, breaking the seal of confession, sexual abuse of a minor by a priest, abuse of authority, homicide, or procuring an abortion. Other crimes can be established by a conference of bishops for a country or by a diocesan bishop for the people within the diocese, but these are very rare.

Some penalties for canonical crimes are imposed automatically, that is, by the very fact of committing the criminal act the person brings down the punishment on him or herself. This right to be judged in accordance with the law relates more directly to the processes for imposing or declaring penalties, either by judicial decision or administrative decree, the two ways of conducting a criminal trial (cc. 1717–1731). Possible penalties include: a reprimand, a work of penance, the suspension of a priest from exercising an office or celebrating the sacraments, an order to reside in a designated place, dismissal from the clerical state, and excommunication (cc. 1331–1333, 1336, 1339–1340).

The main point here is that none of these penalties can be imposed or declared by church authorities except by following the canonical penal process.

ILLUSTRATION

In the aftermath of the scandal of the sexual abuse of minors by priests, the Congregation for the Doctrine of the Faith sometimes resorted to the penal dismissal of priests from the clerical state by papal decree without any trial. The accused priest was not given his "day in court" to defend himself. In some instances the statute of limitations on bringing criminal action had long since run out, and this legal protection was also waived.

In a few cases involving flagrant and repeat offenders, their guilt had already been established in civil court. But in many other cases there was only an allegation of abuse, a "trial in the press," and a preliminary investigation by the diocese. Sometimes the accusers were not interviewed because they had filed a suit for civil damages against the diocese, and then the suit was settled out of court with large awards for the accusers. The case against the priest was sent to the Congregation in Rome, and, without further evidence or even a notification of the accused priest, a decree of penal dismissal was issued.

There is no review possible for such papal decrees, no appeal, and no recourse.

Comment

Permanent dismissal from the clerical state is the ultimate sanction against a priest; it deprives him of both his ministry and his right to support. Because of the extreme seriousness of such "perpetual penalties," the canons expressly state that they cannot be imposed by decree (c. 1342.2). It is clear that some priests were denied a penal process that was in accord with canon law, as promised them by canon 221.3.

III

LIMITATIONS ON AND DEFENSE OF
RIGHTS IN THE CHURCH

WHAT ARE THE LIMITATIONS ON THE EXERCISE OF RIGHTS?

The 1983 Code of Canon Law explicitly names three moderating factors that balance the exercise of the rights of the faithful:

1. the common good of the church,

2. the rights of others, and

3. their own duties toward others (c. 223.1).

These three serve as reasonable reminders that no one's rights in the church are absolute, nor are they to be exercised in isolation, but always with consideration for the community and its members. The three considerations are principles of self-regulation. Individual members of the faithful as well as their groups or associations are to be guided by these factors when exercising their own rights in the church.

The Common Good of the Church

The "common good" is a way of speaking about the purpose or goal of the church, the reason for its existence. The common good transcends the personal goods of the individual members of the church and keeps them in balance, but it is not the same as the institutional or hierarchical good.

The technical meaning of the common good is derived from the encyclicals of Pope John XXIII (*Mater et Magistra*, 1961, and *Pacem in Terris*, 1963) and the Second Vatican Council:

> The common good of society consists in the sum total of those conditions of social life under which human persons are able to pursue their own perfection fully and expeditiously; most of all it consists in the observance of the rights and duties of the human person. (*DH* 6)

In the context of the church, the common good refers to the complex of conditions that facilitate and promote the spiritual development of all of the faithful. It means the array of things that help us to know and follow Christ, to live in his Spirit and make use of the Spirit's gifts. In other words, the common good is the "bigger picture" that we must keep in view so that the church may be an effective instrument of salvation for all.

Since the common good consists in the observance of the rights and duties of the Christian faithful, it functions as a principle of the promotion of rights as well as a factor of limitation on their exercise.

The Rights of Others

It almost goes without saying that we must not insist on our own rights to such an extent that others are deprived of theirs. For example, one group's insistence on its devotion or spiritual exercise should not crowd out other forms of prayer in the local church; or the volume of one person's communications to the people of the parish should not prevent others from posting similar notices in the bulletin; or the extent of one parishioner's service on the parish council should not deny others the opportunity to serve. The rights of the other members of the community set limits on the exercise of our own rights.

Duties toward Others

The responsibilities we have within the community sometimes militate against the free exercise of our own rights. For example, the duty of the chair of a meeting sometimes inhibits her own expression of opinion; or the task of teaching catechism on Sunday morning can cut into one's full participation in Mass or in the social events following it; or my need to care for my young children may stand in the way of my assuming parish leadership roles for which I am well suited. Balancing such duties toward others against the desired exercise of our rights is a common human challenge.

Other Limiting Factors

In addition to these three principles of self-regulation of the exercise of rights in the church community, the canons add an extrinsic limitation. Church authorities are permitted to moderate the exercise of the rights of the faithful in view of the common good (c. 223.2). In other words, when there is a conflict of rights or when the exercise of rights by some threatens to jeopardize the good of the community, then those in leadership roles (bishops, pastors, lay administrators) are charged to direct or modify things to prevent harm to the faithful. If others lose sight of the common good, it is the duty of the leaders to attend to it. For instance, if the number of applicants for places in the parish school jeopardizes its educational task, then it is for the principal or the pastor to figure out an equitable process for limiting the enrollment or expanding the facility.

There are other, implicit considerations when it comes to limits on the exercise of rights in the church. Examples include common sense, physical or moral impossibility, emergency situations, or complete impracticality. Some proposals or programs that are perfectly appropriate for one parish may be entirely out of the question in another. Rights are not absolute, and they must be exercised with the good of the community in mind.

Finally, however, we must recall some guiding principles of the exercise of rights in the church. People are to live together in true justice, in peace and good order, while expressing their rights in harmony. The principle of full freedom is to be preserved in the community. According to this principle, people are to be accorded a maximum of liberty with a minimum of restrictions (*DH* 7).

HOW CAN RIGHTS IN THE CHURCH BE DEFENDED OR VINDICATED?

The Negative Side

"Ay, there's the rub," as Shakespeare's Hamlet exclaimed. The weak link in the rights system of the Catholic Church is the inadequacy of procedures available to vindicate rights. Some means do exist, but their availability and effectiveness are spotty at best.

The need for ways to defend or vindicate the rights of the faithful was evident from the time just after the Second Vatican Council when the work of revising the Code of Canon Law began. In 1967 the international Synod of Bishops approved a set of principles to guide the project. One of the principles stated the need to acknowledge and safeguard the rights of the faithful. Another said that everywhere in the church the need was felt to set up administrative tribunals so that the faithful could defend their rights in them according to proper canonical procedures.

In keeping with those principles, the commission for the revision of the Code developed a system of administrative tribunals for the vindication of personal rights against the arbitrary or unjust exercise of administrative authority. The provision was included in the drafts of the revised Code from 1972 to 1982, at which time it was removed from the final draft.

Pope John Paul II, in his 1983 document of promulgation of the revised Code, said that one of the reasons the Code was needed was so that the mutual relations of the faithful might be regulated according to justice based upon charity, with the rights of individuals well-defined and guaranteed. The Code does define many rights of the faithful, as we have seen above, but their "guarantee" is sadly deficient.

The Code clearly states that "The Christian faithful can legitimately vindicate and defend the rights which they possess in the church in the competent ecclesiastical forum according to the norm of law" (c. 221.1). This canon appears toward the end of the "bill of rights" section of the Code, in the section titled "The Obligations and Rights of All the Christian Faithful" (cc. 208–223). But problems emerge when one tries to find "the competent ecclesiastical forum."

The Catholic Church in the United States, as well as in many other countries, has a functioning *judicial* forum. That is, most dioceses have a working court in which real judges give real justice. The canons regulating these ecclesiastical courts seem to say that rights cases are welcome there: "The object of a trial is the pursuit or vindication of the rights of physical or juridic persons, . . ." (c. 1400.1). "Every right is protected not only by an action [claim], but also by an exception [counter-claim] unless other provision is expressly made" (c. 1491).

The trouble is that "controversies arising from an act of administrative power can be brought only before the superior or before an administrative tribunal" (c. 1400.2). In other words, if you feel aggrieved or believe that your rights have been violated by the action or decision of a church administrator (e.g., pastor, chancellor, bishop), the door of the church's *judicial* forum is closed to you. The diocesan tribunals have no jurisdiction over such matters. It was for such cases that the administrative tribunals were proposed and designed, but they were eliminated from the Code and do not exist. (One administrative tribunal does exist as a part of the Apostolic Signatura, the church's supervisory court in Rome.)

(A technical note: Canonists distinguish "acts of administration," a broader category, from "acts of administrative power," those performed by officials having canonical authority. For example, a school superintendent performs many acts of administration, but he or she may not be acting with the church's canonical power of governance, as, for instance, a diocesan bishop does. In theory these non-canonical acts of administration could be reviewed by the church's judicial tribunals. In practice, they rarely are.)

Most conflicts, grievances, or rights infringements in the church fall into the category of "controversies arising from an act of administrative power." That is, they result from some decision or action on the part of a person in authority, such as a diocesan bishop, vicar general, or parish pastor, who is acting in some administrative capacity. The problems usually arise not from the use of legislative or judicial authority but from the exercise of executive or administrative power (c. 135).

In more personal terms, conflicts in the church usually involve a student being suspended from school, or a group denied use of parish facilities, or a person removed from a ministry, or someone denied a sacrament. Usually someone in authority has taken action, or failed to do so, and someone else, a layperson or someone subject to his or her authority, feels aggrieved by it.

The problem is where to take the grievance. The church courts are closed to the aggrieved person, and the administrative tribunals, designed for just this purpose, do not exist. But there are some other avenues.

The Positive Side

Pope John XXIII, in his 1963 encyclical *Peace on Earth* (*Pacem in Terris*), taught that all human persons are entitled to legal protection of their rights, and that such protection must be effective, unbiased, and strictly just (n. 27). The 1965 council document on *The Church in the Modern World* (*Gaudium et Spes*) also spoke of the need to safeguard the basic rights of all persons under every form of government (GS 29), and this protection of personal rights must be effective and impartial (GS 75). The 1983 Code of Canon Law specifically states that "the Christian faithful can legitimately vindicate and defend the rights which they possess in the church in the competent ecclesiastical forum according to the norm of law" (c. 221.1). Clearly, the defense and vindication of rights is firmly grounded in the church's teaching and law.

In practice, when members of the faithful feel they need to defend or vindicate their rights, there are three paths to take:

1. the gospel path,

2. the path of alternative dispute resolution, and

3. the path of administrative recourse.

The gospel path actually includes the other two paths, and all three begin with the same first step, a direct and personal approach to the person who caused the grievance or violation of rights.

1. The Gospel Path. The gospels are at the center of the church's legacy; their message is precious and perennial. The gospels retain their normative authority in the life of the church, even though they are not "law" in the sense of canon law. The process of conflict resolution and reconciliation described in Matthew's gospel remains valid:

"If another member of the church sins against you, go and point out the fault when the two of you are alone. If the member listens to you, you have regained that one. But if you are not listened to, take one or two others along with you, so that every word may be confirmed by the evidence of two or three witnesses. If the member refuses to listen to them, tell it to the church; and if the offender refuses to listen even to the church, let such a one be to you as a Gentile and a tax collector." (Matt 18:15–17)

The process was surely based on an actual practice within Matthew's church community. It begins with a direct, personal approach, a communication between two Christians. This can be a confrontation or simply a request for reconsideration, oral or written. "Try to understand my point of view. This is why I feel you have wronged me. Please review your decision."

This direct and personal approach is often successful. It can avoid misunderstandings and resolve conflicts. Remember, the vast majority of church leaders are deeply committed, highly motivated persons of good will. They want to act with justice, fairness, and Christian charity.

If, however, this personal approach fails, then some sort of third-party intervention is called for; it could be a friend or someone who is respected by both parties. The person could serve simply as a witness to the claims of both sides, but might more fruitfully serve as a conciliator, or a mediator, or even as an arbitrator.

If this third-party involvement does not produce a satisfactory resolution of the conflict, then the process suggests some sort of hearing or presentation before the local church. In our day, this might be a committee of the parish council or a due process office of the diocese.

Every attempt should be made to settle the matter within the context of the church. Remember the words of the Apostle Paul: "Can it be that there is no one among you wise enough to decide between one believer and another?" (1 Cor 6:5).

2. The Path of Alternative Dispute Resolution. In contemporary North American legal circles, "alternative dispute resolution" refers to alternatives to courtroom litigation, to ways of settling disputes out of court. Typically those means include: (a) conciliation, the use of a mutually acceptable middle-person to bring the disputing parties together and to assist them toward a solution, (b) mediation, wherein a third party acts as a go-between or active promoter of clarification and compromise of issues, or (c) arbitration, when the dispute is given over to an impartial third party who examines the evidence, holds a hearing, and makes a determination that is binding on both parties. These alternative methods are sometimes legally mandated before a judge will accept a case into civil court.

Such alternative processes are very strongly encouraged within the Catholic Church. Matthew quotes Jesus saying, "Come to terms quickly with your accuser while you are on the way to court with him" (Matt 5:25). In that spirit of early reconciliation, the Code of Canon Law repeatedly urges the avoidance of litigation:

- All the Christian faithful, especially bishops, are to strive to avoid litigation among the people of God, and judges are to encourage and assist parties to seek the equitable solution of controversies, even by using mediators or arbitrators (c. 1446).

- In order to avoid judicial contentions, out of court settlements or reconciliations are to be employed, or the controversy may be submitted to arbitration (cc. 1713–1716).

- When persons feel aggrieved by an administrative decision, it is especially desirable that they avoid contention with the author of the decision and try to seek an equitable solution by common counsel, using mediation or some other suitable way of settling the controversy (c. 1733.1).

The Code encourages bishops to set up offices or councils for the purpose of working out the kinds of equitable solutions to disputes suggested above (c. 1733.2). Consequently, many dioceses have offices of due process or courts of equity or grievance procedures, and some of them are active and successful. However, many other dioceses have them "on paper" only, or they are very rarely utilized. Still, these alternative ways of dispute resolution ought to be sought out and used whenever the first attempt, a direct and personal approach, fails.

3. *Administrative Recourse.* Recall that the Code of Canon Law does not permit church courts to hear "controversies arising from an act of administrative power; [they] can be brought only before the superior or before an administrative tribunal" (c. 1400.2). In other words, if you feel that your rights have been violated by a decision of a church administrator (e.g., pastor, chancellor, bishop), the door of the church's *judicial* forum is closed to you. And administrative *tribunals* do not exist at the local level. However, such grievances can be brought "before the superior" of the one who made the decision. That is what is meant by "administrative recourse." It means going to the hierarchical superior of the one who took the administrative action.

The process is outlined in a section of the Code entitled "Recourse Against Administrative Decrees" (cc. 1732–1739; in the Code of Canons of the Eastern Churches, cc. 996–1006). The recourse itself is essentially a request made to the hierarchical superior of the person who made the administrative decision, a request to change or reverse the decision.

But before making this recourse "over the head" of the administrator, the aggrieved person is required to ask the administrator himself or herself to reconsider the decision—in other words, to take that direct and personal first step along the path. The critical point about this initial request to reconsider is that *it must be made within ten days of being notified of the decision* that caused the grievance (c. 1734).

The request to reconsider may be quite short and simple. The petition should contain a request to rescind or change the decision and mention of the harm or injury the decision has caused or will cause. The petition can also include an expression of willingness to submit the matter to conciliation or arbitration, thus opening the door to those possibilities in a timely way. The important thing is to do it promptly, within ten days.

(A technical note: If one makes recourse directly to the diocesan bishop against an administrative act of a person subject to the bishop, such as the vicar general, chancellor, superintendent of schools, or a pastor, then the initial request to reconsider is not required, though it is usually a good idea [c. 1734.3]. But the recourse to the bishop must be made *within fifteen days* of one's being notified of the decision [c. 1737]. For instance, if a person is denied Holy Communion by a pastor, the person who feels her rights have been violated and who is also well aware of the pastor's adamant and often-stated position may have recourse directly to the bishop [within fifteen days of the denial], rather than first trying to get the pastor to change his mind.)

If the recourse is against an administrative decision of the bishop himself, such as a decision to transfer a pastoral associate, then a request to reconsider the decision must be made to the bishop (within ten days), and if he refuses to reconsider it, then recourse may be taken to the bishop's superior, namely the appropriate congregation in Rome within fifteen days of the no-tification of his refusal. The congregations are the offices that assist the pope in his governance of the church; they act in his name and with his authority. Hence they represent a bishop's superior. The recourse may be sent directly to the congregation, or it may be sent to the bishop who is required to transmit it immediately to the proper congregation (c. 1737).

The petition making recourse against an administrative de-cision should include an account of the events that led to the is-suance of the decision and the reasons why the aggrieved party feels the decision should be reversed or altered. A copy of the administrative decision should be enclosed along with any other relevant documents.

The one making the recourse has the right to the assistance of a canonical advocate (c. 1738). Sometimes competent canon-ical counsel can be hard to find. Often those closest to the scene are employed by church authorities involved in the deci-sions being challenged. The Canon Law Society of America (109 North Payne Street, Suite C, Alexandria, VA 22314-2906; 703-739-2560; fax 703-739-2562; coordinator@clsa.org) can suggest the names of available canonists.

The effect of the decision, e.g., the transfer of the associate, is not automatically suspended by making recourse, but a sus-pension may be requested of the superior to whom the recourse is made (c. 1736).

Further details of this administrative recourse procedure may be found in the commentaries on the Code of Canon Law or in some of the articles in the "Further Readings on Rights" section at the end of this book.

The administrative recourse process is officially approved for use throughout the Catholic Church, hence it should be honored by church authorities and faithful alike. It deserves to be better known.

Sources

Codes:

The Code of Canon Law was promulgated by Pope John Paul II for the Western or Latin church on January 25, 1983, to go into effect on November 27, 1983. Of the several versions that are available in English, the best is *Code of Canon Law: Latin-English Edition*, prepared under the auspices of the Canon Law Society of America. Washington, DC: CLSA, 1999.

The Code of Canons of the Eastern Churches was promulgated by Pope John Paul II on October 18, 1990, to go into effect on October 1, 1991. The English version is *Code of Canons of the Eastern Churches: Latin-English Edition*, prepared under the auspices of the Canon Law Society of America. Washington, DC: CLSA, 1992.

Commentaries on the 1983 Code (which also include the canons in English):

New Commentary on the Code of Canon Law, edited by John Beal, James Coriden, and Thomas Green. New York/Mahwah, NJ: Paulist Press, 2000.

The Code of Canon Law: A Text and Commentary, edited by James Coriden, Thomas Green, and Donald Heintschel. New York/Mahwah, NJ: Paulist Press, 1985.

Code of Canon Law Annotated, 2nd edition, edited by Ernest Caparros and Hélène Aubé. Montréal: Wilson & Lafleur, 2004.

The Canon Law, Letter and Spirit: A Practical Guide to the Code of Canon Law, The Canon Law Society of Great Britain and Ireland. Collegeville, MN: Liturgical Press, 1995.

Exegetical Commentary on the Code of Canon Law, edited by A. Marzoa, J. Miras, R. Rodríguez-Ocana. 5 vols. Montreal: Wilson & Lafleur, 2004.

[Note: Editions of the Code of Canon Law and commentaries on it are also available in other languages, such as Spanish, French, Italian, German, and Latin.]

Documents of the Second Vatican Council:

The Documents of Vatican II, edited by Walter Abbott and Joseph Gallagher. New York: Guild Press, 1966.

Vatican Council II: The Conciliar and Postconciliar Documents, revised edition by Austin Flannery. Northport, NY: Costello, 1996.

Documents of the Ecumenical Councils: Volume II, Trent to Vatican II, edited by Norman Tanner. Washington, DC: Georgetown University Press, 1990.

Papal documents and documents of the United States Conference of Catholic Bishops:

These documents are usually published in *Origins*, a weekly documentary service of the Catholic News Service, and later in booklet form by USCCB Publishing, Washington, DC.

Many of these documents also can be found in collections such as *Proclaiming Justice and Peace: Papal Documents from* Rerum Novarum *through* Centesimus Annus, edited by Michael Walsh and Brian Davies. Mystic, CT: Twenty-Third Publications, 1991.

Further Readings on Rights

The Case for Freedom: Human Rights in the Church, edited by James A. Coriden. Washington, DC: Corpus Books, 1969.

A Catholic Bill of Rights, edited by L. Swidler and H. O'Brien. Kansas City, MO: Sheed & Ward, 1988.

John P. Beal:
> "Protecting the Rights of Lay Catholics, *The Jurist* 47:1 (1987) 129–64.
> "The Rights Stuff: Canon Law and the Rights of the Faithful," *New Theology Review* 7:3 (1994) 6–22.
> "Hierarchical Recourse: Procedures at the Local Level," *Proceedings of the Canon Law Society of America* 62 (2000) 93–106.

James A. Coriden:
> "Human Rights in the Church: A Matter of Credibility and Authenticity," *The Church and the Rights of Man, Concilium* 124 (1979) 67–76. New York: Seabury Press, 1979.
> "Toward a New Policy for the Church," *Privacy: A Vanishing Value?* edited by E. Bier, vol. 10 of The Pastoral Psychology Series. New York: Fordham University Press, 1980. Pp. 387–98.
> "A Challenge: Make the Rights Real," *The Jurist* 45 (1985) 1–23.
> "Fair Process," *Authority, Community and Conflict*, edited by M. Kolbenschlag. Kansas City: Sheed & Ward, 1986. Pp. 31–33.

"Alternative Dispute Resolution in the Church," *Proceedings, Canon Law Society of America* 48 (1986) 61–77.

"Reflections on Canonical Rights," *Ius Sequitur Vitam, Law Follows Life*, Studies in Canon Law Presented to Peter J. M. Huizing, edited by J. Provost and K. Walf. Leuven: University Press, 1991. Pp. 21–36.

"What Became of the Bill of Rights," *Proceedings, Canon Law Society of America* 52 (1990) 47–60.

"The Rights of Parishes," *Studia Canonica* 28 (1994) 293–309.

"The Vindication of Parish Rights," *The Jurist* 54:1 (1994) 22–39.

"Freedom of Expression in the Church in the Light of Canon 212 (CIC)," *Proceedings, Canon Law Society of America* 57 (1995) 147–65.

"Church Authority in American Culture: Cases and Observations," *Church Authority in American Culture* (Catholic Common Ground Initiative, Second Cardinal Bernardin Conference). New York: Crossroad, 1999. Pp. 47–61.

"The Right of Catholics to Hold Meetings on Church Property: Canonical and Pastoral Issues," *The Jurist* 62:1 (2002) 76–91.

"Voice of the Faithful and the Rights of Catholics," *New Theology Review* 16:4 (November 2003) 75–78.

Sharon Holland:
"Equality, Dignity and the Rights of the Laity, *The Jurist* 47:1 (1987) 103–28.

Robert J. Kaslyn:
"The Obligations and Rights of All the Christian faithful," and "The Obligations and Rights of the Lay Christian Faithful," *New Commentary on the Code of Canon Law* (cited above).

Protection of the Rights of Persons in the Church: Revised Report of the Canon Law Society of America on the Subject of Due Process. Washington, DC: CLSA, 1991.

James H. Provost:

"Ecclesial Rights," *Proceedings, Canon Law Society of America* 34 (1982) 41–62.

"The Obligations and Rights of All the Christian faithful," and "The Obligations and Rights of the Lay Christian Faithful," *The Code of Canon Law: A Text and Commentary* (cited above).

"Protecting and Promoting the Rights of Christians: Some Implications for Church Structures," *The Jurist* 46 (1986) 289–342.

Due Process in Dioceses in the United States 1970–1985: Report on a Task Force Survey. Washington, DC: CLSA, 1987.

"Human and Legal Rights of Women in the Church," *Women in the Church I*, edited by M. Kolbenschlag. Washington, DC: The Pastoral Press, 1987. Pp. 31–50.

"The Nature of Rights in the Church," *Proceedings, Canon Law Society of America* 53 (1991) 1–18.

"Rights of Persons in the Church," *Catholicism & Liberalism: Contributions to American Public Philosophy*, edited by R. B. Douglas and D. Hollenbach. Cambridge: Cambridge University Press, 1994. Pp. 296–322.

Index

Specific rights discussed in this book are highlighted in bold.

About the Author

James A. Coriden was born in Indiana in 1932. He was ordained a priest of the Diocese of Gary in 1957. He earned a bachelor's degree from Saint Meinrad Seminary, a licentiate in sacred theology and a doctorate in canon law from the Gregorian University in Rome, and a Juris Doctor from the Columbus School of Law at The Catholic University of America.

Fr. Coriden served in the tribunal and chancery of the Diocese of Gary and assisted in several parishes there from 1961 to 1968. He was a member of the faculty of theology at The Catholic University of America from 1968 to 1975, and since that time has taught canon law at the Washington Theological Union, where he is professor of church law and academic dean emeritus.

The author has been an active member of the Canon Law Society of America since 1961. He organized and published several interdisciplinary symposia for the Society and served on its board of governors. The Society granted him its "Role of Law" award in 1987. He was one of the general editors and authors of *The Code of Canon Law: A Text and Commentary* (1985) and the *New Commentary on the Code of Canon Law* (2000), both sponsored by the Society.

Fr. Coriden is the author of *An Introduction to Canon Law* (1991, revised edition, 2004), *The Parish in Catholic Tradition: History, Theology, and Canon Law* (1997), and *Canon Law As Ministry: Freedom and Good Order for the Church* (2000). He has published many articles on canonical topics, especially in the areas of ministry, marriage, teaching authority, and the rights of Catholics in the church.